The Matthew
OF BRISTOL

Bristol Books CIC, 1 Lyons Court, Long Ashton Business Park,
Yanley Lane, Long Ashton, Bristol BS41 9LB

ISBN 9781909446106

The Matthew of Bristol
by Clive Burlton

Published by Bristol Books 2017

Copyright: The Matthew of Bristol Trust

Design: Joe Burt (joe@wildsparkdesign.com)

Clive Burlton has asserted his right under the Copyright, Designs and Patents Act of 1988 to be identified as the author of this work.

All rights reserved. This book may not be reproduced or transmitted in any form or in any means without the prior written consent of the publisher, except by a reviewer who wishes to quote brief passages in connection with a review written in a newspaper or magazine or broadcast on television, radio or on the internet.

A CIP record for this book is available from the British Library

Introduction	9
A slice of history	11
The idea and the project	17
The design	21
The build	27
The launch	35
Skipper appointed, fitting-out begins	39
Sea trials	43
Crew, costumes, logistics and farewells	49
Voyage to Newfoundland	57
Hello Newfoundland and Labrador	77
Nova Scotia and Eastern Seaboard	87
Return leg and homeward bound	91
21st Century *Matthew*	99
About the *Matthew* of Bristol	109

The *Matthew* under full sail in the Irish Sea in 2006

INTRODUCTION

The magnificent wooden ship now berthed at Prince's Wharf in Bristol's Floating Harbour is the 1997 *Matthew* of Bristol, bound for Bonavista in Newfoundland, Canada. She was built to commemorate the 500th anniversary of John Cabot's historic voyage from Bristol on May 2, 1497, that led to the discovery of what we now know as North America.

Lovingly constructed by skilled Bristol shipwrights at Redcliffe Wharf between 1994 and 1996 the *Matthew* is a faithful representation of the medieval caravel type of ship of the same name that was sailed by John Cabot and his 15th century crew during their voyages of exploration.

No ship has ever made a more important discovery than the medieval *Matthew* – a discovery that would change Britain and the world for ever. It gave birth to North America; it sowed the seeds for European settlement and it brought the English language to those shores.

Skip forward 500 years and with a 20th century crew on board, one of the commemorative events in 1997 saw the *Matthew* re-enact the 54-day, 3,000 mile voyage from Bristol and across the same treacherous 'Sea of Darkness' sailed by Cabot. The culmination of years of hard work and endeavour had a huge impact - both in Bristol and in Newfoundland and Canada, where John Cabot is rightly regarded as a founding father.

The *Matthew* receives no public funding and is owned by The Matthew of Bristol Trust – a charity set up for the preservation, maintenance and enhancement of the ship for local and national historic interest, public access, education and training. She's operated by a skipper and 30 enthusiastic volunteers and there's a small office staff to handle administration and bookings. Based in Bristol for much of the year the *Matthew* provides an unrivalled platform to view the city from the water and to absorb what makes Bristol one of Europe's most fascinating maritime cities.

As well as opening a window for discovering part of Bristol's intriguing heritage she goes places; she does things; she's very much a living, breathing ship. The *Matthew* is one of Bristol's most recognisable and well-loved icons and is developing a history all of her own.

But who had the idea to build her? Who ran the project? How was she funded? Who designed her? How was she built? What was it like to sail across the inhospitable North Atlantic Ocean in a tiny little wooden ship?

These and many more questions are answered in the chapters of this book as we uncover the story of the *Matthew* of Bristol. But first, a small slice of history...

The Departure of John and Sebastian Cabot on their First Voyage of Discovery, 1497. Painting by Ernest Board 1906

A SLICE OF HISTORY

Bristol played a major part in transatlantic exploration and between 1480 and 1508 sent a series of expeditions into the Atlantic to search for new lands and trade routes. Of all the many expeditions that sailed from Bristol, John Cabot's voyage aboard the *Matthew* in 1497 was the most famous, as reported in this Elizabethan chronicle:

"This year, on St. John the Baptist's Day [June 24, 1497], the land of America was found by the Merchants of Bristow in a shippe of Bristowe, called the Mathew; the which said ship departed from the port of Bristowe, the second day of May, and came home again the 6th of August next following".

In the later 1400's Bristol merchants were convinced that at some time in the past Bristol mariners had discovered a new land to the West – the Isle of Brasil. Bristol sent out a number of exploratory expeditions into the Atlantic during the latter part of the 15th century to search for this land and its highly valuable brazilwood. The earliest of these expeditions took place sometime before 1476 and at least two more were launched in 1480 and 1481 before the historic transatlantic voyage made by Cabot in 1497.

"Cabot is called the Great Admiral and vast honour is paid to him and he goes dressed in silk, and these English run after him like mad," Said Soncino, Milanese Ambassador to England on August 23, 1497.

John Cabot is believed to have been born in Genoa some time before 1450 but had moved to Venice by the early 1460s, where he became a citizen and merchant known locally by his Venetian name, Zuan Chabboto. Later, he was also known as Giovanni Caboto, the Italian spelling. In 1488 he fled Venice as an insolvent debtor, taking with him his wife Mattea and their three sons Ludivico, Sancio and Sebastian. The family lived in Valencia from 1490 to 1493 where Cabot sought employment as a civil engineer. Here he became known as 'Juan Cabota de Montecalunya'. In 1494 he moved to Seville where he was contracted to build a stone bridge over the Guadalquivir River. Unfortunately the construction of such a bridge proved impossible and following an investigation by the city council, Cabot's contract was terminated. Around the middle of 1495, Cabot left Spain for England, and arrived in London which at that time had a large and influential Italian community in the city.

Now known by the anglicised spelling of his name, John Cabot arrived in England as an ambitious entrepreneur who needed to pay off some fairly hefty debts. Seemingly a smooth talker with financiers and royalty, he managed to convince King Henry VII that he could voyage to find new lands and establish a new and quicker overseas route to the Orient to trade in valuable silks and spices.

Cabot was granted 'letters patent' by the King that stated that Cabot, his heirs and deputies could hold any new lands they found in the name of the King plus receive a monopoly over any trade that they opened up. This meant that others would not be able to muscle in on the trade once it was established without having to incur the early exploration costs. The licence also carried a condition that any subsequent trade that resulted from his expeditions would have to pass through the port of Bristol.

John Cabot used these conditions to convince both

THE MATTHEW

John Cabot leaving Bristol, May 1497. Cabot leaving Bristol on his "Voyage of Discovery".

Sir Humphrey Gilbert taking possession of Newfoundland for Queen Elizabeth at St. John's, August 3, 1583

Bristol merchantmen and Italian bankers based in London to finance his voyage as an investment opportunity. The merchants agreed but only if they were promised a high return on their investment given that it was such a high-risk venture. In view of Cabot's risky financial situation he had little choice but to agree.

Cabot's first attempted voyage in 1496 was unsuccessful. John Day, a Bristol merchant, wrote to fellow explorer Christopher Columbus to say 'Since your Lordship wants information relating to the first voyage, here is what happened: he went with one ship, his crew confused him, he was short of supplies and ran into bad weather, and he decided to turn back.' But his attempt the following year famously succeeded.

On June 24, 1497, Cabot landed in North America, most probably on the island of Newfoundland. He then explored the coast for a month before returning to England in August 1497. Cabot was not the first European to set foot on the island. The Vikings from Iceland, who colonised Greenland in around 1,000 AD, also reached Labrador and the island of Newfoundland. The remains of their settlement, l'Anse aux Meadows, is a World Heritage site.

Although Cabot failed to find a passage to Oriental spices he did discover what would become the highly lucrative cod fisheries off the Eastern North American coasts. He was also the first to draw a map of what is now Canada's East Coast and his landfall has long been associated with giving birth to what would become known as the Americas - and to the introduction of the English language to the continent.

King Henry VII acknowledged Cabot's successful exploration with a reward of £10 to 'hym that found the new isle'. A further reward was made in December 1497 when the King granted Cabot an annual pension or salary of £20. This put Cabot formally and squarely under the King's service and the following year Cabot received permission from the King to charter up to six English ships for a further expedition. King Henry VII also provided loans and one of the ships for the new expedition.

In the event Cabot sailed with five ships, leaving Bristol at the beginning of May, 1498, with provisions for a year. Some of Cabot's financial backers joined the expedition including Brother Giovanni Antonio de Carbonariis, an Augustinian friar from Milan who hoped to bring Christianity to the New World. John Cabot was never seen or heard of again. What happened to him, the ships and their crews remains a mystery.

In the decade after Cabot made landfall, Bristol launched further transatlantic expeditions. In 1499 the Bristol merchant, William Weston, who was a close associate of Cabot, undertook the first English-led expedition to the 'New Founde Land', and was well rewarded by the King as a result. Other prominent Bristol merchants, such as Hugh Elliott and Robert Thorne, led further expeditions there a few years later under a new royal licence. By around 1505 Bristol was the main player in transatlantic voyaging, and even formed the 'Company Adventurers to the New Found Lands' which was dedicated solely to organising further expeditions.

The last Bristol expedition of this era was undertaken by John Cabot's son Sebastian in 1508. By this time it seems that the port's explorers had established that a large continent – America - blocked the route to the Orient. Bristol's merchants considered this land to be of little value, inhabited by what they believed at the time to be primitive people who lived simply and had little worth trading, and so Bristol left the New World to Europe's fishermen.

In 1583 the harbour of St. John's, Newfoundland, was visited by an expedition of four ships commanded by Sir Humphrey Gilbert who carried a commission from Queen Elizabeth to sail the seas and take lands under her banner. Shortly after his arrival Gilbert set up his tent on a hill overlooking St. John's harbour, and caused the masters and chief officers of the ships of all nations there to attend while he solemnly read aloud his commission and formally took possession of the Island in the name of the Queen. Newfoundland thus became England's first possession in North America and her oldest colony.

The settlement of the New Founde Land by the English began 27 years later when Bristol merchant John Guy led a group of 39 colonists who landed at Cuper's Cove (now known as Cupid's Cove) in August 1610. Guy's mission, endorsed by King James I, was to set up a colony for the express purpose of colonising, fortifying, and propagating the settlement for England.

Bristol's long connections with Newfoundland have thus involved its colonisation and settlement as well as its discovery by Cabot and the *Matthew*.

MEMORIALISING CABOT AND DEPICTIONS OF THE MATTHEW

John Cabot's legacy lives on and his story and that of the *Matthew* has been commemorated on both sides of the Atlantic. European exploration of North America began

Cabot Towers were built on Brandon Hill, Bristol (left) and Signal Hill, St John's (right) to commemorate the 400th anniversary of Cabot's discovery

THE MATTHEW

Late 1940s model kit by Hobbies Ltd and a 1911 cigarette card by W.D. & H.O. Wills showing depictions of the *Matthew*

in earnest with Cabot's 1497 expedition and he has iconic status in Canada. On its history website pages, the Canadian Government puts Cabot at the very heart of the country's foundation and the web page includes Ernest Board's 1906 painting of John and Sebastian Cabot's departure from Bristol.

To commemorate the 400th anniversary of Cabot's 1497 discovery, and after Bristol received a gentle prod from the Royal Society of Canada, Cabot Towers were built at both Brandon Hill in Bristol and on Signal Hill, at St John's in Newfoundland. Close links between Bristol and Canada have been forged ever since and in 1912 a civic party from Bristol underlined the connection by attending the unveiling of a Memorial Tower in Halifax, Nova Scotia. The tower commemorated the 250th anniversary of the first 'representative government' in the British Empire in 1758. The civic party presented a gift from the citizens of Bristol in the form of a bronze relief based on Ernest Board's 1906 painting and it was unveiled by the Governor General of the Dominion of Canada on August 15, 1912.

In 1947, the 450th anniversary of Cabot's voyage on the *Matthew* was also commemorated, but in post war Bristol the events were relatively low key affairs and not as visually striking as the ones 50 years earlier. Nonetheless, 'Cabot Day' was held in Bristol on Friday May 2, 1947, and as part of the commemorations, the Professor of Imperial History at Bristol University recorded an account of 'Cabot's great adventure and the discovery of the New World' for radio broadcast on the BBC's West of England Home Service station.

A commemorative service at Bristol Cathedral was attended by members of the public, 28 organisations and 20 schools. During the day school parties inspected paintings of Cabot and his son Sebastian at Bristol City Art Gallery and the Lord Mayor, Alderman Gilbert James, hosted a group

A SLICE OF HISTORY

The *Matthew* model takes pride of place at the Lord Mayor's lunch on May 2, 1947. The model was made for the Imperial Museum of Toronto by Mr J Claridge of Clifton, Bristol

Depictions of the *Matthew* have appeared on several stamps and coins to mark important anniversaries in Canada and Newfoundland

of special guests. These included a representative of the US Embassy, the High Commissioner of Canada, the Trade Commissioner of Newfoundland, the President and Secretary of the Royal Empire Society and Richard Hedke who was the International President of the Rotary Club. The Lord Mayor entertained his guests at a luncheon at The Red Lodge in Park Row where Richard Hedke and his wife were photographed at the lunch inspecting a model of the *Matthew*.

Over the years, several long-standing Bristol institutions including Bristol City Council, Bristol Cathedral and the University of Bristol have used ship imagery in their crests or logos that, on the face of it, might appear to show the medieval *Matthew*. That's probably not the case and the emblems more likely reflect Bristol's maritime heritage; generic medieval ship design and derivations of Bristol's coat of arms that was granted in 1569 and which was based on Bristol seals in use during the 13th and 14th centuries.

Matthew imagery has though been depicted for years and has appeared across many forms, including on Canadian and Newfoundland stamps and coins; on romanticised paintings and drawings; on Royal Doulton pottery; on collectable cigarette cards and on a stained-glass window in St Mary Redcliffe Church in Bristol. It even used to appear as a logo on the front page of the Bristol Evening Post. Nobody knows for sure what the original *Matthew* looked like, but the clues in contemporary sketches of medieval ships and ship-building would have provided at least some basis for these depictions.

15

Martyn Heighton pictured in 2015 on board *Huff of Arklow*

THE IDEA AND THE PROJECT

The idea to build the modern *Matthew* goes back to the early 1980s when Bristol City Council first considered it. However, the idea appeared to flounder and it didn't get any real traction until the aftermath from Bristol's disappointment at coming runner-up to Glasgow in its bid to become European Capital of Culture for 1990. One reason why Glasgow won was that in Bristol's submission, there was an absence of a major showpiece project.

Martyn Heighton, who was Director of Arts at Bristol City Council at the time, had the idea that Bristol should hold such an event at a different date – and resurrected the idea of building a ship to mark the 500th anniversary of John and Sebastian Cabot's voyage to Newfoundland. In Heighton's words, this was a 'dead ringer' for a project, so he wrote and presented a report to the Leisure Services Committee on March 10, 1988.

The report mentioned that for some time, Martyn Heighton and the Acting Chief Executive of Bristol City Council had been considering ways in which this major anniversary might be celebrated - particularly in the light of informal approaches and correspondence from the Government of Newfoundland and Labrador which was showing very significant interest in the looming anniversary. The report suggested that the building of a modern *Matthew* would provide a superb focal point for the 1997 celebrations and if the project was undertaken, the ship could be built within Bristol's historic harbour in full view of the public, and would thus become a tremendous draw both for local people and tourists. The committee paper even included an artist's impression of how the ship building operation might look when viewed from within the harbour. Six years later, the image predicted in the sketch would prove to be an uncannily accurate depiction.

In order to establish historical credibility for such a shipbuilding project, Martyn Heighton had already discussed the outline proposals with the National Maritime Museum at Greenwich. The Museum was very interested and wished to be involved in giving advice on historical matters and in identifying the most suitable naval architect for the scheme.

Financing such a project was a huge challenge. The Government of Newfoundland and Labrador was willing to contribute, but all the costs could not be met and should not be met from the other side of the North Atlantic Ocean. Building the ship in full view of the public itself could provide additional revenues although further funds would still be necessary and it was important to develop a strategy to meet all the costs.

It was envisaged that should a modern *Matthew* be built, she would be sailed to Newfoundland in the summer of 1997 in time for St John's Day and Cabot Day. She would return to Bristol which would be her 'home port' some time later, possibly as deck cargo on board a merchant ship. At this stage, there was no thought that the ship would make a return voyage across the Atlantic Ocean.

The 1997 Cabot 500 celebrations themselves would need financial support and in view of the importance of the event, the report recommended that a Special Advisory Committee be formed to bring together interested parties from the business community, the media, English Tourist

THE MATTHEW

Colin Mudie with his plans for the *Matthew*

Board, and other relevant bodies to form a partnership with Bristol City Council.

The report concluded that if Bristol City Council wished to proceed with the proposals, it was vital that action be taken as soon as possible - the lead-in time for establishing an Advisory Committee, securing the finances and researching the design of the ship would be around two to three years.

Apart from one dissenting voice – Councillor Rumble voted against the proposals – the Leisure Services Committee approved the recommendations for the 1997 Cabot 500 celebrations and the proposal was welcomed and endorsed at a subsequent meeting of the full city council. Bristol was about to embark on a flagship project that would be nine years in the making.

Shortly after the decision to proceed was made, Councillor Derek Tedder, the then Lord Mayor of Bristol, led a small civic delegation which included Bunty Wilcox, Master of the Society of Merchant Venturers, and Martyn Heighton to St John's, Newfoundland, on June 24, 1988 - timed to coincide with St John's Day and Cabot Day. The Government of Newfoundland and Labrador used the visit to propel plans for its own Cabot 500 celebrations, and the civic party returned to Bristol with a $5,000 grant from the Newfoundland and Labrador Government to help fund the costs of a naval architect to research and design a modern day vessel that resembled as closely as possible the medieval *Matthew* sailed by Cabot.

Following a short selection process, where presentations were received from three other applicants, Colin Mudie, one of Britain's most celebrated and well-respected naval architects and yacht designers, was appointed by Bristol City Council. For the architect behind hundreds of ship and boat-building projects, designing a modern-day *Matthew* would be a revelation and an opportunity not to be missed.

Although the initial funds had been provided to start work on the design, it would be another two years before the infrastructure was in place to allow the project to get underway.

In 1990, Bristol City Council and the Bristol Chamber of Commerce & Initiative formed 'Bristol 97' which was the trading name of Bristol Cabot 500 Celebrations (1997) Ltd – a joint venture company formed to celebrate the 500th anniversary of John Cabot's historic voyage to Newfoundland from Bristol and to organise the construction of a ship based on Cabot's medieval *Matthew*.

Other Bristol-based organisations including the Civic Society, the local Trades Union Council and the Society of Merchant Venturers all lent their support to the project.

Early in 1991, St John Hartnell, a successful property surveyor, auctioneer, businessman and member of the Society of Merchant Venturers, was approached by Councillor Graham Robertson, the leader of Bristol City Council, to see if he would chair the joint venture company. It was a challenge he could not refuse and over the following 12 months he gradually formulated the plans and put

THE IDEA AND THE PROJECT

together a team to bring this ambitious project to fruition.

His Royal Highness, The Prince Philip, Duke of Edinburgh agreed to be Patron to the project which he saw as one commemorating the quincentenary of the start of the Colonies, the start of the Commonwealth and the start of the spread of the English spoken language.

Sir John Wills was invited to be the President of the project and Peter Workman joined the company as Director General. The Bristol 97 office was located in Clifton. With plenty of financial and operational challenges ahead, the team visited the Festival of the Sea in Brest, France, in 1992. They came away with the idea that Bristol should hold a similar International Festival of the Sea in 1996 – with the aim of supporting the *Matthew* building project and raising awareness in the ship. Adding more weight and underlying the importance to which Canada regarded the 500th anniversary, the Canadian High Commissioner in London, Frederik Eaton, wrote to the project office late in 1992. He stressed the importance of the anniversary in Canada's history and that the voyage of the modern *Matthew* in 1997 would symbolise the strong and affectionate links between Canada and Great Britain. He wished the project every success and hoped that the people of Bristol would lend it as much enthusiasm as the people of Newfoundland would show on the arrival of the modern *Matthew* on Canadian shores. No pressure there then...!

Although Bristol City Council could support the project in an advisory capacity and provide staff time without charge, it was unable to make any cash contributions. Money for the project had to be raised through the private sector and through sponsorship and donations. Several local businesses including Barclays Bank, British Rail, Wessex Water, British Gas, Bristol Water and South Western Electricity Board all chipped-in with welcome contributions totalling around £50,000 during 1993, but the amount

The Project Team. Left to right: Peter Workman, Georgina Bird, Anne Baldwin-Charles, Michael Blackwell, St John Hartnell, Sara Hartnell, David Redfern and John Bremmer

was not material. So, St. John Hartnell used his contacts in the property development business and all his powers of persuasion to bring a backer on board. In the end it was an old friend, Michael Slade, a keen yachtsman, who agreed to underwrite the project through property development company Helical Bar plc – the company Slade headed. Slade needed to persuade his board that this was a good thing for Helical Bar's shareholders. He did just that, and on November 17, 1993, John Southwell, Chairman of Helical Bar along with Slade and Financial Director, Nigel McNair-Scott came to Bristol to make the formal announcement.

Helical Bar not only agreed to fund the cost of the new *Matthew*, but also agreed to underwrite the entire cost of the International Festival of the Sea in Bristol in 1996 – with the estimated cost of both approaching £3 million.

Slade's arrival, and the backing of Helical Bar, provided the impetus and the financial clout that enabled St John Hartnell to kick start the project, and with Colin Mudie properly appointed, the research and the ship design process could start in earnest.

15th century model of the *Mataro* on display at the Maritime Museum, Rotterdam

THE DESIGN

Colin Mudie set about his task in a typically robust, logical and structured manner. He wasn't an archaeologist or a historian and so the design process he instigated followed a very practical regime common to modern, 1990s naval architecture.

Helped by his wife, Rosemary, Mudie started by examining the evidence and what was known about the original ship; what was known about Cabot and what was known about the 1497 voyage.

The medieval *Matthew* was built towards the end of the 15th century in a period of rapid development in ocean-going ship design and immediately before naval architecture in any formal mathematical sense came into being. North Atlantic exploration and voyaging was well practiced and a great body of knowledge and experience had built up by the time of the medieval *Matthew* – especially in the trading port of Bristol.

Sailing ships, along with cathedrals and castles, were the most complex pieces of construction of pre-industrial times. For thousands of years, the ship combined technical complexity with versatility in a way that was not matched until the development of the steam engine. Sailing ships were the top technologies of their time and were built by the best engineers of the age to meet the needs of commerce or war. By the time the medieval *Matthew* was built at the end of the 15th century, even quite modest ships of the period had become complex pieces of machinery. Thousands of pieces of timber and hundreds of feet of rope were combined in such a way that the final structure could withstand the stresses and strains of around 20-30 years of hard work. Even in the 1990s, designing and building the modern *Matthew* was a complex and skilful exercise.

Marine historians form an impression of old vessels from three main sources – written accounts, contemporary pictures, sketches or paintings and archaeological wrecks. For the *Matthew*, there was no contemporary illustration and no wreck of a 15th century caravel had yet been found. However, in 2002, and nine years too late for Mudie's study, most of the timber hull of a 15th century sailing vessel known as the 'Newport Ship' was discovered on the west bank of the River Usk in Wales.

Mudie had vast experience of designing everything from small sailing boats to huge motor yachts and had designed a wide variety of other replica craft – or 'reconstructions' as he preferred to call them. These included a Greek trireme (an ancient warship with oars), a Viking longboat and a small

The hull of King Henry VIII's flagship, the *Mary Rose*, at Portsmouth

THE MATTHEW

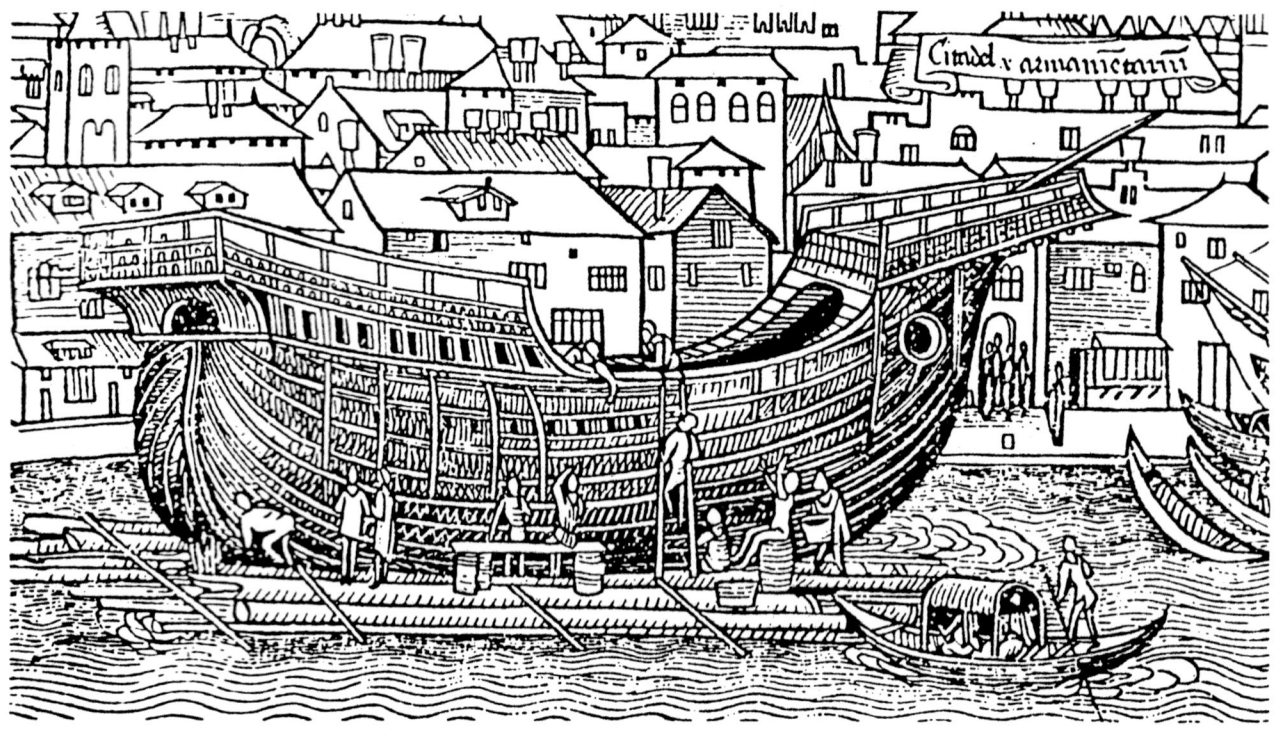

Sketch from the 1483 book, *Die Reise ins Heilige Land*, showing medieval shipbuilding from a float.

open boat, the *Brendan*, which was based on a vessel that St Brendan is reputed to have sailed across the Atlantic in the sixth century.

Mudie's brief was to design a faithful copy of the *Matthew* that could sail swiftly and safely across the inhospitable North Atlantic Ocean. Despite the absence of plans, pictures or sketches of the original *Matthew*, it was still possible to define quite closely what it would have been like. Mudie had already gathered information on what was known about the original *Matthew*, what was known about John Cabot and what was known about the original 1497 voyage.

Analysis of these facts helped to inform Mudie's study of the many contemporary writings and illustrations made of medieval vessels and to test out his hypothesis. He also examined one of the oldest and most famous 15th century models of a caravel – the *Mataró* - which is on display in the Maritime Museum in Rotterdam in the Netherlands. Mudie believed that the contemporary illustrations and the model of the *Mataró* would have been made for knowledgeable audiences and that the details they contained could be taken seriously. He also studied the hull of King Henry VIII's Tudor flagship, the *Mary Rose* that was raised in 1982 and is now on show in Portsmouth. For Mudie, understanding some of the details of how the *Mary Rose* was built cleared up a few questions when studying the contemporary illustrations of

THE DESIGN

German woodcut sketch showing the stern of a caravel and the triangular lateen-sail, 1486.

Woodcut sketch of early 16th century caravel from *Libre de cosolat tractat dels fets maritims*, Barcelona 1502.

medieval ships and shipbuilding.

Armed with all this information and historical detective work, Mudie now knew a lot more about how the original *Matthew* would have looked and how she would have sailed.

He was ready to consult more widely on his assumptions and conclusions and in March 1993 he circulated his findings to naval historians and others. He asked for feedback and for authoritative comments and corrections before his designs for the modern *Matthew* were too far advanced.

Mudie's first assumption was that the ship was built or bought by an experienced mariner who intended to sail west across the cold and stormy waters of the North Atlantic Ocean into uncharted regions. The original *Matthew* would also have needed to be self-contained for as long as a year.

His next assumption was that she was a strong, weatherly, sea-going vessel and reasonably easy for the crew themselves to maintain. The original *Matthew* sailed from Bristol down the notorious Bristol Channel where the tides run very strongly – especially in the upper reaches and off headlands. The original *Matthew* would therefore have been

THE MATTHEW

An illustration of shipbuilding in the Middle Ages, published in the Nuremberg Chronicle in 1493.

as good at sailing towards the prevailing wind as any ship of the period. She would also have been able to dry out without risk of damage in case she ran aground and hence may have had a reasonably shallow draft. Ships using Bristol harbour were subjected to constant stresses and strains as they dried out at every low water, so the original *Matthew* could be expected to be well built from good quality materials. Away from harbour, ships relied on their sailing ability, but sailing ships are at their most vulnerable in light and failing winds while sailing close to the shore. So, to navigate safely up and down the Bristol Channel, the original *Matthew* would have carried the largest practicable sail area.

Mudie's next assumption concerned supplies and storage capacity. The tonnage of the original *Matthew* is known from historical records and if Cabot was considering what he thought might be a 9,000 mile voyage to Japan, then Mudie assumed he was planning for a voyage of around six months. To calculate the volume of the hull, Mudie worked out what would have been required to carry supplies for the crew for a long period at sea. Sailors in the 15th century did not have the benefit of tinned and frozen food and their diet was basic but bulky. In the early weeks of a passage, there would be a decent supply of livestock to provide fresh milk, eggs and meat. Mudie worked on the assumption that the original *Matthew* carried around eight tons of food – enough for six months – and enough water for around three months as this could be replenished much more easily than food. In addition, Mudie calculated that the vessel at sea would require spare rigging and sails; replacement anchor rope; replacement timbers and spars; two landing boats and room for sufficient booty and trade goods to make the voyage financially viable. Consideration of all these factors led Mudie to believe that a hull with an overall length of slightly more than 60 feet and a beam of around 20 feet would provide the necessary capacity and void space.

The shape of the hull was Mudie's next consideration and it was the *Mary Rose* that provided the best clues to the underwater shape of the original *Matthew*. Built around ten years after the original *Matthew*, the *Mary Rose* had a hull form that surprised Mudie in its sophistication for the period. The shape of its hull was very close to what scientists have developed to optimise 'laminar flow' and to create 'lift'. To a ship designer this means, first, ensuring that the movement of water past the hull is as smooth and undisturbed as possible and, second, designing the hull to create 'lift', much like an aircraft's wing. This was important in helping the boat sail closer to the wind and to reduce leeway – ie the downwind 'slippage' through the water when a boat tries to sail into the wind. With ships like the caravel, the leeway would have been 15 to 20 degrees and even more in heavy weather. Mudie was incredibly impressed with the hull of the *Mary Rose*, and it had a major influence on his design of the underwater sections of the modern *Matthew*.

THE DESIGN

The last major assumption concerned the rig. Mudie had to choose between a lateen and a square rig. The caravel was thought to have originated in the Mediterranean with the sails originally modelled on the Arabian Dhow, the early versions of which carried lateen sails. However, it seemed clear to Mudie that the square sail was eventually preferred for exploration work. For example, when Christopher Columbus sailed the Atlantic in 1492 he was so disappointed in the performance of *Niňa* (one of the two lateen-rigged caravels on the expedition and originally called the *Santa Clara*) that when he arrived in the Canary Islands, he had the masts and spars cut down and rearranged as a square rig. Mudie also consulted the contemporary illustrations of Bartolomeu Dias. When Dias returned to Lisbon in 1488 from his caravel voyaging, he chose to build vessels for exploration purposes that were three-masted, square rigged on the fore and main masts and lateen rigged on the mizzen. Mudie also noted that the three-masted rig of this kind was the normal seagoing rig in England at this time.

Mudie's report was well received among respected academics and naval historians. He made a few tweaks to his designs following helpful feedback from people like Dr Basil Greenhill, former Director of the National Maritime Museum and former Chairman of the *SS Great Britain* project, and Luis de Guimaraes Lobato, a caravel expert at Aporvela, the Portuguese Association of Sail Training. Mudie also consulted George Woollard, an experienced Bristol Channel Pilot, who gave advice on what attributes a modern *Matthew* would require in order to successfully negotiate the Bristol Channel. It was also suggested to Mudie that if he followed the illustrations in the Hastings manuscripts of 1450, he wouldn't go far wrong.

Consultation over, by February 1994 Mudie's initial line plans and most of the architectural drawings behind Design Number 395 were ready.

MATTHEW
1997

DESIGN NUMBER 395

Each of Colin Mudie's drawings contained the same signature emblem above. With 394 designs to his name before the *Matthew*, he was one of the most respected maritime architects in the country. In an interview in 1995 he commented:

"It's a big detective story and a big assembly of the logic that would have applied to a ship exploring out of the Bristol Channel. We know that she was 50 tons because that's recorded and we can translate that into a general size; we know she had 18 crew and by making up watch bills for different rigs we can be fairly certain she had a rig just like this – a square rig rather than the alternative lateen rig. We also know she sailed the Bristol Channel, therefore we can tell she had a certain degree of manoeuvrability and this all comes back to a vessel of this general size and rig."

THE BUILD

Appointed during 1993, the task of interpreting around 40 architectural drawings, recruiting the shipwrights and project managing the construction was handed to Mike Blackwell – a vastly experienced marine surveyor, consultant and designer. One of his first tasks was to prepare a budget for the building costs. His initial estimates for a two-year build came out at around £750,000 including approximately £350,000 for labour and £105,000 for materials.

A Bristol boy originally, his career had taken him around the world, before fetching him back up on the shores of his home city. Blackwell explained in a magazine interview where he had developed the skills that would lead him to managing a project that came along once in a lifetime, "I served my apprenticeship as a boy in my father's business. This was back in 1948, on the river between Keynsham and Bristol when everything was wood – everyone in the boating business worked in wood in those days."

After spending some time at Bristol's Charles Hill & Sons shipbuilders (which closed in 1977) and working in West Africa, the West Indies, in Italy for 12 years as manager at the Aga Khan's shipyard in Sardinia which catered for the super-rich, and then in Kuwait, he finally decided, "I'm coming home again. And I did so right in the middle of a depressed – no, a non-existent – UK shipbuilding industry and I started working for Lloyds underwriters and insurance companies, making damage and repair reports."

Blackwell said he was chosen for the modern *Matthew* project because, "Although there are about 50 people still working in Britain who had the right experience for the job, I was a Bristolian which was of some importance. And I could put a team together. Many of 'The Boys' (he always referred to them as 'The Boys', despite the decade or three which separated most of them from short trousers) I had known since I was a boy, and some of them I knew from looking around as an insurance surveyor, finding people to do capable and competent work for insurance companies. I chose the most able from the whole field around Bristol and asked them to join." And so they did.

Dozens of other shipwright's from across the country, keen to be involved in a unique project, sent their CVs in for consideration, but were ultimately unsuccessful. Blackwell's 'Boys' – average age of 42 - were the lucky ones and although they knew how to build wooden boats, building a reconstruction of the medieval *Matthew* would prove to be a novel and rewarding experience for all of them. At an

Mural painted by local school children on hoardings around the construction site

27

THE MATTHEW

hourly rate of £14, the pay wasn't necessarily generous, but it wasn't too bad either. Ten men were engaged on site initially, with a maximum of 12 employed at peak workloads, reducing to nine towards the end of construction.

Although unable to supply the project with hard cash, Bristol City Council provided the quayside land on which the modern *Matthew* could be built. Two years of rent-free land use in the centre of Bristol Harbour was quite a contribution - and what a wonderful symbolic space it was. The modern *Matthew* would be built on Redcliffe Wharf; possibly just a few hundred metres from where the original *Matthew* may have been built, and directly in the early morning shadow of the magnificent medieval church of St Mary Redcliffe. Known as the 'Mariner's Church', it has long been associated with the medieval *Matthew*'s adventures. In St John's Chapel hangs a whalebone reputed to have been brought back to Bristol on the *Matthew*; there's a stained glass window showing John Cabot, his sons, and the brave little ship and there's a wooden model of the *Matthew* perched on a stone shelf within the church.

The weight of history was not lost on Mike Blackwell and his 'Boys' as they set about their work...

Blackwell and two of his team started work at Redcliffe Wharf on February 7, 1994 – a typically dark, dank and dreary winter's day in Bristol. Initial tasks involved the clearing of the site and renovating outbuildings for use as workshops and a site office. During the month, other nearby facilities came on stream including empty warehousing space in Winterstoke Road, Ashton, and a covered yard in Gas Ferry Road, near to the home of the

View of the centre line (the keel) with stem post and stern post now attached

THE BUILD

Another view of the frames taking shape – looking like the ribs of a beached whale.

SS Great Britain. The warehouse was supplied with a generator and 120 sheets of plywood were laid across its floor. The plywood was then painted black in preparation for using the warehouse floor as a 'lofting' space where the ship's frames or ribs could be fabricated. Here, full-sized templates would be drawn using Mudie's plans before each was made accurately on the floor, before being trucked to Redcliffe Wharf for assembly. The Gas Ferry Road yard was used mainly for the preparation of the keel.

Mike Blackwell must have enjoyed his trip to a timber merchant in Hull on March 1, 1994, where he purchased an African opepe tree measuring 15 inches x 12 inches x 50 feet long and weighing a massive 1.5 tonnes. The tree would form the keel of the new *Matthew* and is the backbone of a ship, running from the bow to the stern. By tradition, for a wooden vessel like the *Matthew*, it would be cut from a single piece of mature oak. But today's trees do not have the stature of their 15th century ancestors, so African opepe was used as a modern substitute. Originally, mature oak trees which fell on the Longleat Estate during the Great Storm of 1987 were earmarked for the ship. But the Longleat oaks were used to rebuild St George's Hall at Windsor Castle following the fire there in 1992.

The modern *Matthew* was built completely out of unseasoned green timber, which went against conventional practice. There wasn't the time to go looking around

MATTHEW VISITOR CENTRE

Above the shipwrights an attractive steel-framed, wave-effect canopy was built to keep the site dry. It also provided space underneath for a Visitor Centre where school parties and others could witness, first hand, the construction of the first seagoing vessel built in Bristol Docks since the 1,541 tonne tanker *Miranda Guinness* in 1976. The Visitor Centre also contained 'The John Cabot 500 Exhibition' that included interpretation panels and education packs for visiting schools, for use in the study of the Tudor period. Souvenirs could be bought in the Visitor Centre shop and the site was enclosed by 100 feet of hoardings painted by pupils from the St Mary Redcliffe and Temple Schools. The giant mural depicted Cabot's dramatic voyage across the Atlantic, the Bristol Channel and the coast of Newfoundland and of course the medieval *Matthew*... surrounded by sea monsters! The Visitor Centre also included a Radio Room set up by local amateur radio enthusiasts who manned the site during construction. A special call-sign, GB500JC, was issued to radio 'hams' who wished to keep in touch with the building work.

The Duke of Edinburgh about to 'tap' the keel on May 20, 1994

the country for the best trees, grown to the required shape. Sometimes trees had to be bought and used immediately including English oak acquired from forests in Gloucestershire and Hampshire. The modern consensus was that timber should mature but the wood used for the modern *Matthew* was as green as grass and soaking wet. As each component was prepared, it was coated with linseed oil and turpentine to seal in the moisture and prevent the wood from drying too quickly. The opepe keel arrived on site on March 10, 1994, and was laid across wooden blocks at Redcliffe Wharf to allow the shipwrights access to the whole length so that they could start their work. This is where the *Matthew* would be built and the blocks were high enough to allow the shipwrights to work underneath and to drive the planking up when the time came. At each end of the centre line, ie the keel, the shipwrights fashioned the stem and stern posts in sections and out of solid pieces of oak – their joinery skills coming to the fore as they put together the complex inter-locking skeleton.

For the shipwrights, to use wood in such a way was a challenge and a pleasure as Mark Rolt explained at the time.

THE BUILD

"I think the beauty of wooden ship-building now is that most of the people who do it are really interested whereas 500 years ago I don't think they necessarily were – it was just a job. We are used to taking apart and rebuilding wooden ships, but the beauty of this is there are no rusty nails, there's no rotten pieces of wood, and it's all new, which is just bliss – a completely new experience!"

What the shipwrights probably didn't bargain for was the amount of attention from the media and members of the public which grew significantly as the shape of the ship emerged on the quayside and in full view of passers-by. News crews, documentary makers, radio reporters, newspaper journalists and press photographers all wanted a piece of the action - and in the days before digital cameras, the IPhone and social media, the Bristol public and visitors from further afield happily snapped away on their instamatic cameras and recorded proceedings on their camcorders.

By mid-May 1994, the keel was ready to be 'laid' – which is the formal and traditional recognition of the start of a ship's construction. It is often marked with a ceremony attended by dignitaries and the owners of the ship. One such ceremony took place on Redcliffe Wharf on May 20, 1994, where the patron of the project, HRH the Prince Philip, Duke of Edinburgh was on hand to do the honours. After landing by helicopter on College Green, he arrived at Redcliffe Wharf in the Lord Mayor's horse-drawn carriage. He unveiled a plaque and used St John Hartnell's auctioneer's gavel to tap the keel, which was then blessed by the Bishop of Bristol. Around 200 guests attended the event including the Deputy High Commissioner for Canada and the Italian Ambassador to Britain. In the evening, the Lord Mayor of Bristol hosted a reception at the Mansion House to acknowledge the achievements so far.

The following morning, the shipwrights could get back to their work and the 30 or so frames or ribs started

The oak frames being assembled and fitted by the shipwrights

to arrive from Winterstoke Road and were fitted to the keel over the coming months. The overall shape of the vessel was now emerging and at night, silhouetted against powerful lighting, the oak frames of the modern *Matthew* stood out like the ribs of a giant beached whale.

Next step was the fitting of an inner keel, or 'keelson' which ran above the main keel and was bolted through, securing the bottom sections of the frames. The frames were then cross-braced with beams on which the decking

Inner keelson fitted to frames

Planking shaped and fitted to the frames

would later be laid and the beams were fixed in position with huge oak brackets known as 'knees' – each carefully fitted by hand. The strength of a wooden ship depends not only on the size of the timbers but also on the perfect fit of each individual piece, which is glued and through-bolted to 'lock' the framework into an incredibly strong structure. The final job before planking the hull and decks was fitting the 'wales'. These were four-inch long square oak timbers that ran the length of the outside of the hull – again, their purpose was to lock the frame of the ship into a single, sturdy structure.

Up until this point, construction had gone pretty smoothly, but fitting the wales presented a serious problem to the shipwrights. Mudie had designed a stern that was rounded. This shape required the massive timbers to be bent around in a tight curve – a much tighter curve than the wood could normally be expected to accommodate. The traditional technique for curving timbers is literally to 'cook' them in a makeshift steam oven – and that's exactly what the shipwrights on Redcliffe Wharf did. A massive steam box was fabricated and used with a Calor gas water heater. The whole system bubbled away for hours at a time. As the timbers warmed up in the hot, moist atmosphere they became flexible and could be bent easily. Once out of the steamer, the shipwrights only had a few minutes to get the 'steamed wale' into position and clamped before the timber cooled and went stiff again. Judging by the expletives that could be heard above the sound of hammering, the process was intensely frustrating for the shipwrights! A few pieces snapped before they succeeded in getting the timbers fitted to their satisfaction. Even with the wales in place, 2½ inch thick pine planking still had to be coaxed around the problematic stern – a task that proved to be one of the biggest challenges in building the modern *Matthew*.

The final shape of the ship was sometimes changed during the building and Blackwell's 'Boys' had to confront practical problems on a daily basis. Unusual points of construction were worked out within the team using years of practical experience. Often, the team would get several ideas on how to solve a particular problem. They would debate it and then call Colin Mudie to discuss the solution – he'd often agree with their suggestions and then they'd

THE BUILD

The completed hull ready for launch

The proud construction team. Front, left to right: Neil Blake, Andy King, Alan Wood, Douglas Doule, Steve Blake. Back, left to right: Warwick Moreton, Brian Cumby, Denis Williams, John Douglas, Mike Blackwell, Tim Miles, Peter Williams and Robert Williams. Missing was Mark Rolt.

carry out the work.

Trial and error is how it would have almost certainly been with the original *Matthew*. It would have been one of the last ships to be built before naval architecture became a recognised profession under the Elizabethans.

Mike Blackwell believed that his 'Boys' would have built the hull in pretty much the same way as the shipwrights who built the original *Matthew*. In 1497, there would have been many more shipwrights and they would have used hand saws, hand planes, and adzes – in 1995 power saws, planes, hand saws, adzes, hand planes and fewer men were involved. Summing up this phase of the build he said, "One of the things we have come to believe is that the old ships were built the way we have done it. We don't think the old shipyards had the money to stockpile wood so the foreman would make the templates, then choose the trees by eye. We may not be rediscovering old skills, but it is knowledge which has been lying dormant over the years until we came along."

The final job before launching was to make the hull watertight – a constant pre-occupation with all boat builders. The basic techniques that are used to 'caulk' a hull have not changed in hundreds of years. The hull of the modern *Matthew* is a carvel construction, namely where planking is laid edge to edge and a small gap of around ¼ inch is left between each plank. Before a vessel can be launched these gaps have to be filled or caulked, which is a laborious process. First, caulking cotton or oakum is gently hammered into the seam using a broad, chisel-shaped tool called a caulking iron. Next, a stopping compound is trowelled over the seams and smoothed flush with the rest of the hull. When a wooden boat is launched it usually leaks at first, but once the caulking and the planks get wet, they swell - sealing the hull against further leaks.

The modern *Matthew* was caulked using oakum (fibres unpicked from old rope) and covered with tar. By September 1995 it was ready for its maiden splash...

Robert Bibbings aged 6, sitting on an 18th century naval gun that was fired as the *Matthew* entered the water

THE LAUNCH

As with most projects, it is the meticulous and often unseen attention to detail that determines a successful outcome. The planning for the modern *Matthew*'s first contact with River Avon water was no different and started some nine months earlier with technical assessments from Colin Mudie and prospective contractors on how an estimated 50 tons of dead weight could be manoeuvred safely into the water. Discussions were also held with Denis Williams – foreman and shipwright who was in charge of every launch from Charles Hill & Sons' shipyard between 1958 and 1976. This was a big deal and needed some clever and experienced thinking.

Two options were considered – crane launching or side launching. The latter with a 10-fold difference in cost and potentially more risky, was soon discounted. City council engineers and archaeologists surveyed Redcliffe Wharf once the crane launch option had been chosen. The site was once the manufacturing home of Bristol Blue Glass and had been loosely packed and infilled with rubble over the years. The potential for ground subsidence and the impact on quayside masonry were the main points of concern. Once these had been addressed and solutions discussed – and the £8,000 crane-hire cost agreed – the scene was set for the launch party. And what a party it was.

On the eve of the launch, the Lord Mayor of Bristol hosted a dinner at the Mansion House to mark the occasion. Sandwiched between arrival drinks and dinner, guests viewed a short play about Cabot's historic voyage.

The following day, the launch of the modern *Matthew* was an elaborate affair. The morning of the launch, Saturday September 9, 1995, was bright and clear, much to everyone's delight. The flags and the bunting fluttered in the stiff westerly wind and the bedecked vessel looked a picture. The site had been prepared over the previous week and a few days before the launch, the *Matthew* was carefully inched towards the edge of the harbour wall. The manoeuvre took 20 men eight hours to complete. Now she was ready for the spectacle.

It was an important day for the people of Bristol who had watched 'their' little ship grow from a pile of timber to something resembling a medieval vessel. Around 20,000 people lined the quays and nearly 2,000 more filled temporary stands on Redcliffe Bridge and Redcliffe Way. Representatives from more than 30 media organisations were on hand to record the proceedings and the air was full of excitement as a flotilla of little boats near the quay tooted

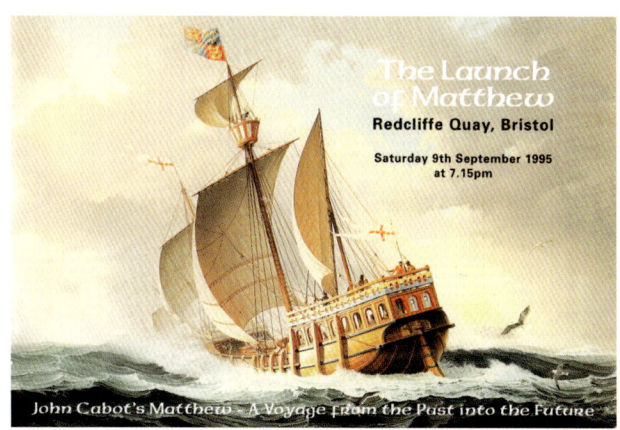

Front cover of the programme for the launch ceremony

THE MATTHEW

horns. Many people from Newfoundland and Labrador attended and among the crowd was Alan Cabot, 87, from Vancouver – reported by the press to be a descendant of Louis Cabot - one of John Cabot's sons.

As the crowds jostled for the best views and the guests took their seats, the Avon District Sea Cadets got things underway with a marching and musical performance with a seafaring flavour. Next up was a 30-minute set by the Band of the Welsh Guards; songs by the Filton Male Voice Choir and the Choir of St Mary Redcliffe Church, and a service led by the Bishop of Bristol.

Finally, the big moment came. Accompanied by the City of Bristol Trumpeters, Lady Wills (wife of Sir John Wills) cut the ribbon and officially launched and named the modern *Matthew* with a bottle of Harveys Bristol Cream sherry – as opposed to the traditional bottle of French champagne. This went down well in Bristol.

The day belonged to Mike Blackwell and his 'Boys' - resplendent in their new sets of white overalls. Once the bottle of Bristol sherry had been broken over the bows, Mike

THE LAUNCH

Final preparations before the launch ceremony

The *Matthew* about to make its maiden splash

Blackwell gave the signal... and 43 tons of African opepe, English oak and Douglas fir was lifted high above Redcliffe Wharf and lowered gently into the murky waters of Bristol Harbour.

Amid the cheering and applause, the playing of Land of Hope and Glory and the deafening explosions from an 18 cannon gun-salute, a nervous figure shrouded in white clambered on board and hastily checked the bilge. Five minutes later a relieved Mike Blackwell re-appeared to announce that the hull was tight with only a small amount of water infiltration – exactly as expected.

As the bells of St Mary Redcliffe Church rang out to signal the end of the ceremony and the start of another chapter in the city's maritime history, the guests who had paid £10 for a grandstand view of the launch, made their way to the £75 per-head Matthew Ball which was taking place nearby. With a dozen or so marquees covering the entire centre of Queen Square in Bristol, the Ball ticket included a champagne reception, dinner and wine, a nightclub, dancing to live bands and side-shows and entertainments.

The launch and the Ball were key milestones. They marked an important stage in the construction and raised the profile of the project in the local, national and international media. It was also important to signal to Bristol's friends across the North Atlantic that the City's Cabot 500 celebrations were on track to run in tandem with those in Newfoundland and Labrador. For the organisers and financial backers of the *Matthew* project, the launch and the Ball also provided an opportunity to entice more sponsors to participate in the funding of the project.

The following afternoon felt very much like 'after the Lord Mayor's show', but work had to be done. With a heavy head or two from the night before, the shipbuilding team lifted the modern *Matthew* quietly and unceremoniously back on to Redcliffe Wharf. The long process of fitting out the inside of the ship and building the superstructure above the hull began. Although the basic hull was finished and she had floated for the first time, there was still around six months of painstaking work ahead to turn her into a seaworthy ship capable of sailing the North Atlantic.

SKIPPER APPOINTED, FITTING-OUT BEGINS

Although round-the-world sailor Sir Robin Knox-Johnston was the bookies favourite to become the first skipper of the modern *Matthew*, it was another accomplished and experienced sailor, David Alan-Williams, who got the master's berth.

He joined the *Matthew* project in July 1995, shortly after returning from San Diego, California, where he was a member of the victorious New Zealand America's Cup team. In 1994, he crewed for Sir Peter Blake and Knox-Johnston on *Enza New Zealand* which sailed around the world in a record breaking 74 days, 22 hours and 18 minutes. With 140,000 ocean sailing miles under his belt – and many voyages in high latitudes, strong winds, big seas and in the proximity of even bigger icebergs – David Alan-Williams clearly knew his stuff. But he also knew that sailing the modern *Matthew* would be totally different from anything he'd done before.

He soon became acquainted with Mike Blackwell and the shipwrights and attended the launch event. David Alan-Williams's input to the fitting out of the ship would be an essential part of the process – after all, he would skipper the ship across the North Atlantic and back. His first impressions of the work at Redcliffe Wharf were very positive as he explained at the time, "I've just come back from Newfoundland and they tell me that when we arrive there on June 24, 1997, we'll certainly be passing icebergs so it's re-assuring to see the depths of her timbers and that she's a stout ship. She's going to sail well. She won't be skipping across the waves – but we'll be going at a sedate, ladylike pace."

One of his first jobs, however, was to get to work on crew selection and he set out his requirements. As far as the general laws of the ship were concerned, enthusiasm to play an active role in all operations; participation in the spirit of life aboard a 'medieval' ship; the physical and mental ability to climb to the 'crow's nest' unaided and some musical/singing talent were all high on the list of desired attributes. Oh, and definitely no smoking could be allowed on board a wooden sailing ship!

There were 18 places up for grabs and he was looking for a range of sailing skills. Prior to the voyage to Bonavista, he'd like the crew to have been on two passages with a minimum of ten days sailing on the new ship. He also wanted a mix of sailing skills – highly experienced sailors who had completed trans-ocean passages under sail; generally competent sailors who were used to coastal and inshore passages and were competent at sail handling and helming; and trainees who were fit and eager to learn and participate. He thought

David Alan-Williams interviewed on deck shortly after being appointed

THE MATTHEW

there could be a division of around ⅓ from each of these categories.

Back to the fitting out and the pressure was on. A few days after the launch, the main mast arrived at Redcliffe Wharf in order to be 'fashioned'. Hewn from a solid pine trunk more than four feet in diameter, it would take the shipwrights three months to turn the mast from a square to a round section. The castles were built and decked over and two small cabins were constructed aft – a small chartroom and the skipper's cabin. The interior was fitted out with 18 bunks for the crew and a galley was built with a large oven and refrigerator. A huge bank of batteries powered the latest in electronic navigation equipment and was charged by a 160 horse powered diesel engine with hydraulic drives to operate the propellers. Essential compromises in the building of a medieval representation, the modern *Matthew* would not have been granted the necessary certification and permissions from the Marine Safety Agency without navigational aids and an engine.

The colour scheme was also subject to scrutiny to ensure as an authentic a finish as possible. It was agreed that the ship had to be presented as a clean new vessel worth a million pounds and a proper representative of Bristol and that she should not be given any artificial ageing to represent antiquity. Stained glass windows in houses of the period were studied and these showed that bright painted decoration was prominent and commonplace in medieval and Elizabethan England. Colour samples of reds, blues and yellows were produced for paint manufacturers to match as closely as possible. The forecastle rails were to be painted yellow (upper plank) and blue (lower plank) and the aft castle rails yellow (upper plank) and blue (lower plank) with roundel carvings picked out in red. The colour scheme was provided to William Bishop who had been commissioned by the Society of Merchant Venturers to paint an oil on canvas

The stern of the ship looking very similar to her medieval cousins

depiction of the modern *Matthew*. Subsequent research has found that the correct livery of the Tudors was, in fact, green and white – the colours in use on the ship today.

Nearing the end of its fitting-out, another landmark day in the story of the modern *Matthew* was on February 26, 1996, when the ship was once again lowered into the water via a crane hoist. It said farewell to its quayside home as everything else that needed to be completed from then on would be done on the water.

With another ceremony looming, the following day the

ship's mast, fashioned from a 75 foot Douglas fir, was lowered into place. A 500-year-old 'good luck' gold coin struck during Cabot's lifetime was placed underneath the mast. More than 100 people gathered to watch Lord Mayor Joan McLaren perform the centuries-old 'stepping out' ceremony. The 22 carat coin, called an 'Angel', was minted in 1496 and featured a Tudor rose and the coat of arms of Henry VII. It also depicted the Archangel Michael slaying a dragon and was worn in the Middle Ages as a good luck charm. The coin was presented by Bristol solicitor, Mike Rendell, who bought the coin in the 1980s. The 'Angel', valued at six shillings and six pence, was used to pay lawyer's fees throughout the Middle Ages, so had very appropriate maritime and legal connections. Speaking at the ceremony, Mike Rendell said, "It's nice to think that wherever the *Matthew* goes, the coin will go with her and hopefully bring luck to those who sail in her."

Ceremony over and with the main mast 'stepped', it was time to complete the fitting out. Over the following weeks the fore and mizzen masts were stepped, the rigging was completed and the sails attached and hoisted for the first time. A crow's nest made of oak and flying the pennant of Henry VII was also fitted to the main mast. The *Matthew* completed a day of engine trials in Bristol Harbour on March 24, 1996, and she was now ready for her trial by sea and for a great day in Bristol's history.

Sunday March 24, 1996, was a day of mixed emotions. For Mike Blackwell and the 'Boys' who built the ship, it was the end of two years involvement and a day of pride and sadness. The shipwrights joined the temporary crew on the ship's first outing along the Avon Gorge. With cans of celebratory beer in hand, a number on board spoke to the media. Brian Cumby, was one: "It was very romantic when we headed up the Gorge in the morning mist – I felt it was the culmination of two years hard work. It was wonderful to see so many people turn out to see us. And the people of Bristol

Mike Rendell and a close up of the 1496 'Angel' that sits under the main mast

really seem to have taken the *Matthew* to their hearts."

Final word from Mike Blackwell: "It's been a super occasion for me but it was a bit sad as well because my day to day involvement is coming to an end. Everything has so far gone according to plan and now the fate of the *Matthew* is out of my hands." Blackwell was keen for there to be more work for the shipwrights and wondered whether there might be a revival in Bristol shipbuilding. He was a member of the Board of Trustees for the Underfall Yard which was being turned back into a working shipyard. "That, when we get the funds to be up and running, will be a good facility which might keep ship repairing going in Bristol – and, of course, this might lead on to building."

The *Matthew* pictured during sea trials off Weymouth and Portland

SEA TRIALS

The ship's first outing was a short one. She headed out of the Cumberland Basin and under the Clifton Suspension Bridge. Hundreds of people lined the dockside, the Portway and the Suspension Bridge, many of them carrying cameras and camcorders to record the moment for posterity. The ship rounded the next bend in the river, turned around and sailed back to Redcliffe Wharf.

Skipper David Alan-Williams hailed her first journey a success. "I feel as if we have been blessed. It is very unusual for an easterly wind to blow along the Gorge, but it happened just as we were approaching the Clifton Suspension Bridge. When we dropped the main sail I really felt that the adventure was beginning. Nothing like this has been attempted for 500 years. So far I am very impressed with the way she manoeuvres."

Even though the modern *Matthew* had been formally 'handed over', when she left Bristol on Wednesday, March 27, 1996, four of the shipwrights, including Mark Rolt and Brian Cumby, were still on board. There was much finishing off work to be done on the maiden voyage to London and the shipwrights worked daily between 8am and 5pm. The rest of the crew were split into port and starboard watches and sailed the ship three hours on, three hours off at night and four hours on and four hours off during the day. One would steer, two were on look-out and the watch-leader would navigate.

Rodney North, one of the volunteer crew on board, described those early sea trial days and the ship's first venture into the Bristol Channel... "Once out in the Severn Estuary, partial sail was set but the wind was slight and we had to press on with the motor running. By Lundy, the wind had increased slightly so the fore-course was set, but it wasn't until we rounded Land's End that the wind freed and we were able to set all sails and bowl along at about five knots steady as a rock with just a slight heel – no engine and blessed peace!"

Having finished the bulk of their work, most of the shipwrights were dropped off at Falmouth before the ship arrived at Weymouth on March 31, 1996, to be greeted by another crew, this time from the BBC children's TV programme, Blue Peter. Presenter Stuart Miles interviewed some on board who were now being joined progressively by crew who would sail on the 1997 adventure.

Following a few days of trials around Portland, where the rigging was put through its paces, the modern *Matthew* continued her easterly passage along the English Channel

Blue Peter presenter Stuart Miles interviewing crew member Nigel Church

43

THE MATTHEW

SEA TRIALS

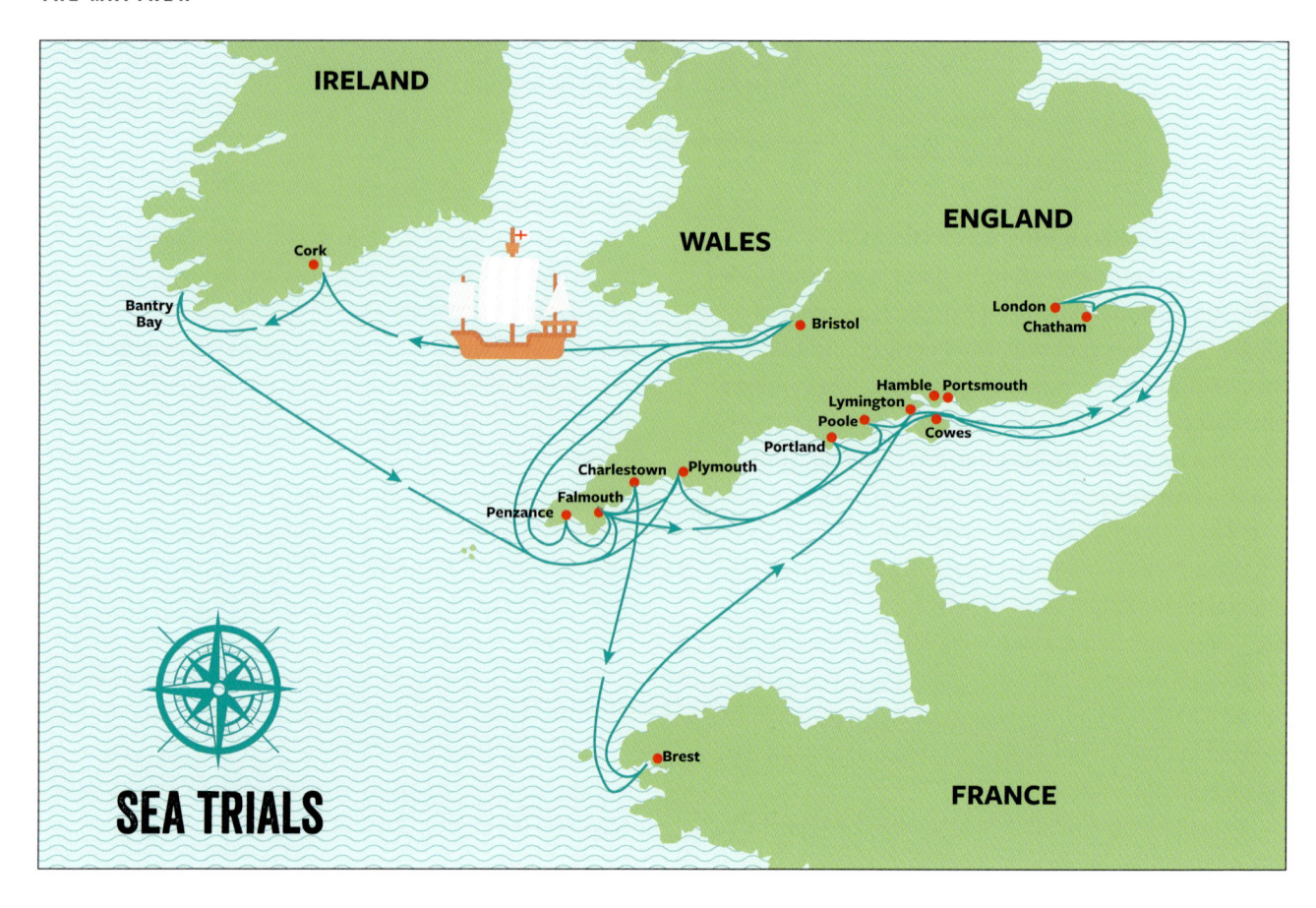

taking in Poole and then Lymington where she met an old friend. The ship's designer, and local resident, Colin Mudie hopped on board and was keenly interested in how the *Matthew* was performing under sail. Next up was Cowes and Brighton and a few days later the ship made its way up the Thames Estuary towards the centre of London. The opening of Tower Bridge to let her through was quite a sight for the city's commuters. She arrived at Canary Wharf in time for a reception in the appropriately named Cabot Place where Michael Slade was on hand to promote the Festival of the Sea to a gathering of business leaders and to attract more financial backers for the ship. He was keen to recoup some of the monies expended by Helical Bar and was pleased that the Canadian Government had agreed to charter the *Matthew* for several weeks in 1997. This would help recoup some of the costs. The ebullient Canadian High Commissioner, Royce Frith QC, was also present and with a glint in his eye had this to say whilst stood next to the ship, "I've been to Bristol and I think that the awareness that Bristol has of its role in the founding of Canada is not widely enough known. And that is why I salute everyone here for what they are doing to make sure that happens."

Formalities over, and with a few more financial backers secured, the crew prepared for the return voyage to Bristol and to continue to test the performance of the rigging and the sails and how the below deck accommodation arrangements were working. It took four weeks for the return journey with several days earmarked for public visits, public relations, television appearances and documentary filming. In Portsmouth, the ship was on parade in the docks for St George's Day and then completed another phase of sea trials around Portland. The passage from Portland to Bristol took in Plymouth and Penzance before arrival back at Redcliffe Wharf in Bristol on May 15, 1996 – in time for the start of the International Festival of the Sea.

Called 'Bristol 96', the Festival was the biggest ever celebration of Britain's maritime history and was held over four days at the end of May. Attended by 368,000 people, it really put Bristol on the map. The Floating Harbour hosted around 700 classic and traditional craft – from tall ships to steamers, and from yachts to trawlers – to celebrate 500 years of exploration and endeavour at sea, and, of course, the completion of the modern *Matthew*, which was the centre-piece of the Festival. Proceedings got underway on May 24, 1996, when Kermit the Frog of the Muppets and Sir Robin Knox-Johnston fired a cannon from the deck of HMS *Rose* - an 18th century frigate.

The same day saw the formation of The Matthew Society – established by enthusiasts following an idea by Steve Isaac. Interested in the modern *Matthew* story and the history of John Cabot and medieval voyages of discovery, the membership of the Society soon grew to more than 300 with members from the UK, the US and Newfoundland. Although not part of the formal management structure or involved in the running of the ship, keen subscribers became actively and enthusiastically involved in all things *Matthew* for many years.

Michael Slade sharing a joke with Miss Piggy. The Muppets were in Bristol promoting the European premier of their film, 'Muppet Treasure Island'

St John Hartnell receiving a cheque from Les Owen, CEO Sun Life Assurance Society

On the last day of the Festival, the *Matthew* motored down the Avon and sailed off to continue her sea trials. Leading a flotilla of tall ships, she was bound for another Festival of Sail at Bantry Bay in Ireland. As the fleet headed out into the Bristol Channel, the skies turned grey and soon strong winds whipped up a nasty sea. It was a tough time for all the boats and the modern *Matthew* was forced to shelter

THE MATTHEW

The wooden crow's nest was replaced with a lighter fibreglass version

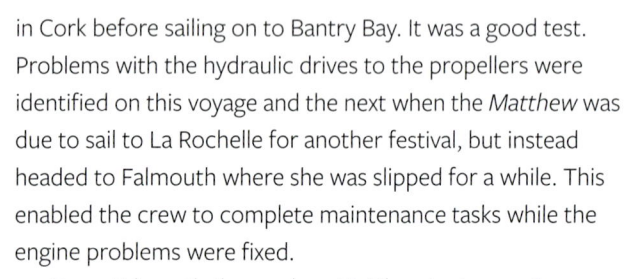

The ship during her extensive re-fit on the Hamble

in Cork before sailing on to Bantry Bay. It was a good test. Problems with the hydraulic drives to the propellers were identified on this voyage and the next when the *Matthew* was due to sail to La Rochelle for another festival, but instead headed to Falmouth where she was slipped for a while. This enabled the crew to complete maintenance tasks while the engine problems were fixed.

From Falmouth the modern *Matthew* had several appointments in Cornwall including the West Cornwall Maritime Festival in Penzance, the Helford River at Falmouth and a BBC TV documentary appearance in Charlestown before she headed off to France for the 'Brest 96' Festival in July 1996. Next up was a passage from Brest to the English Channel for participation in Cowes Week in early August. This was her last public appearance in 1996 and afterwards she went into a boatyard on the Hamble for a comprehensive refit.

The unpopular drive units were replaced by more conventional hydraulic gearboxes. The rudder was altered to improve her handling and the masts were removed and lightened to improve stability. Also designed to improve stability in rough seas, some of the lead ballast was removed from the hold and was attached underneath the keel. The oak crow's nest was replaced with a lighter fibreglass version. The rigging was overhauled and all working systems were checked and double-checked. The ship had originally been varnished. Although she looked elegant, varnish was not a tough coating and ropes rubbing on the ship's timbers had produced ugly marks. So the exterior was laboriously sanded down to bare wood and dozens of coats of a special Norwegian oil treatment were applied by several Matthew Society volunteers who worked at the weekends. The oil had the effect of bringing out the full, rich colours of the timbers, which now looked magnificent. The living accommodation was also stripped out and rebuilt to an improved design. The refit (the list for which ran to 26 pages) was expensive and put even greater stresses on the finances of the project. However, crucially, it increased the safety of the ship and provided the crew with better living conditions.

The ship was relaunched from the Hamble at the end of November 1996 and voyaged to Plymouth where it was met

Some of the crew and Matthew Society volunteers celebrate the Courage sponsorship with a few cans of Directors Bitter

by several Matthew Society volunteers who carried out odd jobs and helped crew the ship back to Bristol where it arrived at Redcliffe Wharf on Sunday, December 8, 1996. The lessons learnt from the summer sea trials and the modifications made during the extensive re-fit meant that the modern *Matthew* was ready to take on the full might of the North Atlantic.

Before then though, she had other important tasks to perform. Back to where she was built, she was laid up and went into tourist mode – attracting hundreds of people to clamber on board and visit the Visitor Information Centre over the chilly winter months. The ship also doubled-up as a floating restaurant and below deck was turned into a candlelit dining room for up to 14 people, while there was space on deck to cater for cocktail parties serving 40. Income generation and the work to attract sponsors continued unabated and the project received a major boost when Bristol-based brewery Courage wrote a cheque for £100,000. As well as providing branded sweatshirts for the crew, the company marked its sponsorship by brewing a special cask ale called 'Navigator' – a barrel of which was delivered to the ship in traditional fashion by a horse-drawn dray.

Thousands of people watch the *Matthew* as she leaves Bristol at Cumberland Lock

CREW, COSTUMES, LOGISTICS AND FAREWELLS

For the voyage to Newfoundland the core crew was to be appointed from those who had sailed during the sea trials in 1996. Recruitment of the crew continued after the ship was laid up for the winter at Redcliffe Wharf and the skipper was keen to fill some very specific positions – two Watch Leaders, Navigator, Cook, Medic, Commissar, Shipwright, Rigger, Sail Maker, Mechanical/Electrical Engineer, Diver, Entertainments Officer, Musicians, two Camera Crew for stills and film, Bristolians and Newfoundlanders – and, of course, plenty of Grommets (medieval term for able-bodied sailors). For further authenticity with John Cabot's day, someone from Burgundy and a barber (ship's surgeon) from Genoa would do nicely!

The anticipated age of the crew was 18 to 25-years-old. That aim was thrown off course with the appointment of John Jack Smith from Ottawa, a Master Mariner who was a mere 77 years of age! The youngest, aged just 20, was James Roy from Lymington, whose occupation was given as 'boat bum'. In the end, the crew was made up of six from Bristol and surrounding area; three from Hampshire; two from the South East; two from Newfoundland; two from Canada; one from Tasmania; one from New Zealand; one from Ireland and one from North Wales – average age, 36.

The crew was expected to help during a ship maintenance and familiarisation programme in March 1997 and to be on board during two weeks of 'shake-down' trials in early April. April 1, 1997 was the first time that the voyage crew spent a night at sea together and the final passage from Weymouth to Bristol helped them to get familiar with the ship and with each other. There was much mirth on board when the Bristol Evening Post ran a story about the crew being replaced by a multi-national and half male/half female crew – with representatives solely from all 16 European Union nations. It was a timely April fool's joke and only temporarily caused a stir!

Whilst in the Weymouth Bay area, the ship was on the slip at the old Royal Naval base at Portland. A final complete check was made to ensure all the underwater planking and caulking was sound – and this was surveyed by Mike Blackwell and an inspector from the Marine Safety Agency. After applying four coats of antifouling, the Blue Peter children's TV programme again filmed the *Matthew* – this time sliding back in to the water.

Over the Easter weekend, the ship and her crew, who were joining daily from their jobs, sailed out of Weymouth

Crew members getting to grips with needle, thread and rope challenges

THE MATTHEW

The crew, the support team and Michael Slade during the survival course at Warsash

David Redfern (back), Gerry Gibbs (left) and Terry Nash preparing lunch

taking aboard family, friends, sponsors and the media. With plenty of drills, raising and lowering sails, manoeuvring the ship, mooring, towing, anchoring and navigating in and out of harbour in fog, it was excellent practice and training for the fledgling crew.

Man-over-board routines were practiced with the retrieval of buckets thrown into the sea and one of the crew donned a wet-suit and jumped into the swell to test the crew's ability in a live situation. Nothing was left to chance with preparing for the voyage and the experience of a lifetime. Shortly before leaving, the whole crew attended a sea survival course at Warsash Maritime Academy in Southampton.

The shore team, who also attended the Warsash course, had also been busy preparing for the big day. In overall charge of shore support and logistics was John Bremner with Lawrence Freeman in charge of the technical and systems side of things. Media Manager David Redfern was busily drafting press releases and marshalling journalists, news crews and documentary makers. Laurel Alan-Williams, the captain's wife, was in charge of food and provisions for the 7½ week passage to Newfoundland. With 19 hungry men on board, enough food for 57 meals a day or 3,078 meals between Bristol and Bonavista had to be sourced. The food, designed to deliver 5,500+ calories per person per day, was packed into weekly boxes that were lashed to the hull beneath the bunks. The main hold would be home for all the crew apart from the skipper. In here were 18 canvas bunks racked two-high along each side of the hull plus two more in the centre. Within each bunk space each crew member had to store all his clothes and equipment and find room to sleep.

Water tanks below the floorboards could store enough water for a week's supply for drinking and cooking. By a process of reverse osmosis, the on-board water maker

CREW, COSTUMES, LOGISTICS AND FAREWELLS

could convert salty sea water into fresh drinking water. Operated off the main engine at the same time as charging the batteries, 40 litres of fresh water could be produced every hour. Cabot would have been envious as, on a medieval ship, much of the main hold space would have been used to store barrels of water, or rather, weak ale beer as fresh water goes brackish very quickly when left to stand. Also stowed on board the modern *Matthew* was a traditional wooden cask, filled with brandy for the voyage – a present from The Matthew Society. This would come in handy sooner than expected.

Another gift, skilfully carved and painted by Matthew Society member Paul Hatch, was a figurehead of a Talbot hunting dog. The symbol of good luck was fitted under the beak of the forecastle. Figureheads in medieval times would have been small if anything at all. Just like the wheel to steer by, it was another century or more before figureheads of buxom women graced the stems of sailing ships.

Laurel Alan-Williams was also in charge of clothing. She had painstakingly researched the clothing and fashions of the late Gothic, Renaissance and Baroque periods and consulted manuscripts on how to make Tudor stage costumes. Her designs were as authentic for medieval clothing as Colin Mudie's were for medieval ships. Local company Alexandra Workwear used her designs to produce a full set of clothing for each member of the crew. The crew also made their own additions to customise these and other pieces of clothing made specially. As well as friends and family making clothes at home, there developed a community of helpers during the month or so before departure, busy as bees measuring; taking in; adjusting; stitching up; adding buttons and pieces of leather. Paper templates were made to help the production team with the making of shirts, berets, bonnets and caps – all with "The Good Ship *Matthew*" label sewn inside. Guided by Laurel

The crew model their medieval clothing for the first time in a photocall on board ship on April 8, 1997

Alan-Williams's designs and led by the tenacious energy of Jean Fletcher (Secretary to The Matthew Society), the team at the Redcliffe Wharf sewing room was 17-strong, with another 13 people also helping from home.

The ship's crew was called together aboard the modern *Matthew* in early April 1997 for a photo call and proudly modelled their new medieval costumes. Not designed specifically for general use on deck, they certainly looked the part. The period clothing theme was also taken up by many others involved with the project before the ship departed.

Whilst at Redcliffe Wharf, the ship had another visitor - Chief Mi'sel Joe of the Micmac Indian tribe. He came aboard and was curious and pleased to see and share in the atmosphere of the celebrations of a voyage that had a huge impact on North America and his people's ancestors. The significance was not lost on Chief Joe, but rather than dwell on the past and lament the changes and impact of European settlement on native Indians, he conveyed an acceptance of history. The Micmacs came to Takemukek, as they named Newfoundland, when there were already other tribes living

THE MATTHEW

Dressed in Tilley clothing and wearing Matthew ties, the crew say farewell to Redcliffe Wharf. Front, left to right: Orlando Stuart, Nick Craig, Paul Venton, Gerry Gibbs, Mark Chislett, Matthew Wills, Chris LeGrow, Back, left to right: Rev Russell Owen, Kevin O'Leary, Steve Greenwood, Luke Porter, Terry Nash, David Alan-Williams, Russell Thiessen, James Roy, Peter Zimonjic, Nigel Church and John Jack Smith. Missing was Martin Pick.

there. He presented a paddle to the crew of *Matthew* as a gesture of goodwill between people travelling by water. It would be returned on arrival in Bonavista.

As well as medieval clothing, the crew was also supplied with Tilley hats, shirts and trousers – traditional Canadian outdoor clothing - that they wore to a service at St Mary Redcliffe Church on May 1, 1997, to mark the departure of the modern *Matthew* from Redcliffe Wharf. It was traditional in medieval times for departing sailors to visit the shrine to Our Lady in the North Porch of the church before setting off on their voyages. During the service, a large candle was lit that would stay alight for the duration of the voyage. The service was attended by families of the crew, Matthew Project staff, friends, volunteers and Matthew Society members.

It was quite a day – as it was right across the country. It was General Election day and at Westminster the political landscape was just about to change. With a huge 10% swing in its favour, the Labour Party was on course to oust John Major's Conservative Government and gain power for the first time in nearly 18 years.

Meanwhile, back at Redcliffe Church, service over, the

CREW, COSTUMES, LOGISTICS AND FAREWELLS

Daybreak on May 2, 1997 – a beautiful day in Bristol

A proud moment for Mike Blackwell and Rosemary and Colin Mudie

crew led the procession to the ship. Then with family and friends on board the first small part of the voyage began as the modern *Matthew* cast off her shore lines at Redcliffe Wharf and passed through the Prince Street swing bridge before being tied up at the Cannon's Marsh Amphitheatre – in readiness for security checks for the following day's Royal visit and send off. The General Election result meant that the Queen couldn't come to Bristol to see off the *Matthew* in person. Instead she had matters of State to attend to and needed to be present at Buckingham Palace for the first audience with her new Prime Minister – a beaming, and fresh-faced Tony Blair.

The crew was up early on May 2, 1997. A 6am start saw them cleaning the ship for the day's events. Another day, another service. This time at Bristol Cathedral where the gathering congregation of around 1,000 people were greeted by music from the Newfoundland and Ottawa Youth Orchestras. The processions were accompanied by a fanfare from the City of Bristol Trumpeters. It was a major civic occasion with the City Swordbearer, the Lord Mayor, the High Sheriff and the Lord Lieutenant all in attendance along with representatives from across the pond including Brian Tobin, the premier of Newfoundland and Labrador. The Queen was ably represented by project patron HRH Duke of Edinburgh.

At the end of the service the civic party, VIPs and members of the congregation walked the short distance to Bristol Harbour and stood alongside the modern *Matthew* where the crew, in their medieval clothing, were formally blessed by the Lord Bishop. The Duke of Edinburgh presented David Alan-Williams with a bible signed by Her Majesty and then took the helm for a short while as the *Matthew* made its way to the Cumberland Basin lock. Guests now departed, the crew could continue loading stores of fresh vegetables and Enza apples and tested out the newly cast and mounted swivel guns. In the evening, friends and family came aboard for a final meal with the crew before departure.

However, the farewell events were not quite over and there was another extravaganza in town. The departure of the *Matthew* coincided with the Goram Fayre in Avon Gorge. According to medieval mythology the Avon Gorge

THE MATTHEW

was constructed by two giants – the brothers Goram and Vincent. Apparently, Goram fell asleep, only to be accidentally killed by Vincent's pickaxe. Any excuse for a party. A two-mile stretch of the Portway beneath the Clifton Suspension Bridge was full of exhibition marquees; marching bands; buskers; dance groups, street theatres and entertainers and there were three stages for local radio stations and performers. The Royal Marines were also in town – attempting a record-breaking 'Commando Slide' across the Gorge.

The centrepiece event for the weekend was, of course, the departure of the *Matthew*. At 15.30 on Saturday, May 3, 1997, the ship left Cumberland Basin lock for the third leg of the voyage. As she came out of the lock, towed by the rowing cutters from *HMS Victory*, *Cutty Sark* and the *Atlantic Challenge*, the four swivel guns on board roared into action. There was an equal response from the thousands of people all along the banks of the River Avon. At 16.25, just as the ship's bow came under Brunel's Clifton Suspension Bridge, another Bristol icon, Concorde, flew overhead – right on cue – as if symbolising the staggering technical advances since the medieval *Matthew*'s journey into the 'Sea of Darkness' 500 years earlier.

All four guns on the *Matthew* blasted out in unison giving a deafening echo as the sound burst off the cliffs of Avon Gorge. In response a world record Cracker Roll of a million firecrackers was fired from the Clifton Suspension Bridge. Bidding farewell to the rowing cutters, the display sail was set and the ship proceeded down river, accompanied by the soft tones of the Bristol Cathedral Choir as the Goram Fayre was left behind.

Being flown on the *Matthew* on this leg of the journey was a pilot flag that was handed over at Pill to mark the 500th anniversary of the first pilot's licence being granted to Charles Rey of Pill. In return, a Pill Sharks pilot flag was

David Alan-Williams, the Duke of Edinburgh and, in the background, John Jack Smith and Newfoundland and Labrador Premier, Brian Tobin

The *Matthew* leaving Bristol behind and passing the Goram Fayre

CREW, COSTUMES, LOGISTICS AND FAREWELLS

taken on board for the voyage, to be presented when the ship arrived in Newfoundland. At the Royal Portbury dock, volunteers Ron Bond and Rodney North were on hand to take on board the last of the food boxes. The *Matthew* was laid up here for the night and during the evening the crew were guests of honour at the Matthew 500 Ball attended by 2,000 people and hosted by the Bristol Port Company. Profits from the evening were due to go to the John Cabot Matthew Trust that had been formed under the chairmanship of Jay Tidmarsh, to create a fund to ensure that the modern *Matthew* remained in Bristol after its return from Newfoundland – and was used by the citizens of Bristol to help promote Bristol's image around the world.

The Ball started with an 8pm champagne reception, followed by dinner and toasts to the Queen and the *Matthew*. At 10pm the band of the Royal Marines from Plymouth played for half an hour and at 10.30pm sharp, the crew boarded the ship. With cannons firing and with fireworks overhead, it really was time to say farewell and to start the journey of a lifetime...

In the middle of the
North Atlantic Ocean

VOYAGE TO NEWFOUNDLAND

After the parties and the celebrations from the night before, it was now reality on a damp, blustery and grey Bristol Channel morning. One of the tasks on leaving Portbury Dock at 8.30am on May 4, 1997, was to ensure the ship's log – the record of important events in the management, operation, and navigation of the ship – was completed every day. These were communicated to the shore-based team by an impressive array of 1990s technology.

During John Cabot's time in the 15th century, when a ship left port, there was no means of contact or getting information of its whereabouts. In contrast, 20th century *Matthew* had a sophisticated satellite communications system supplied by Stratos, a Newfoundland company that was arguably the equal of the system on the Apollo 1 spacecraft. The system would allow telephone and fax contact from on board, and David Redfern, back in Bristol, was geared up to co-ordinate the messages to and from the ship. There were also two Satcom terminals used for tracking the ship and for sending telex and email messages. Stratos would plot and monitor the route of the ship across the Atlantic and these positions were to be relayed to the Matthew website at the John Cabot City Technology College in Bristol for marking up on a plotting chart. The daily log reports from the ship were sent back via satellite to the website managed by Lawrence Freeman. Students at the College (now called John Cabot Academy) worked with their teacher, Bryan Berry, to edit the many questions that were sent in and then sent a few choice ones to the crew to answer and put these on the website. As it cost money to send every character and punctuation mark via satellite there was no direct access to the ship – in any case, there wouldn't be time to sail the ship and to reply to the messages. Only the ship's business information, messages from the crew's immediate family and information on the weather were sent on – and these had to be no more than 60 characters per line and edited down to half a page per crew member every few days or so. Weather analysis and routing information was provided for *Matthew*'s voyage by Lee and George who worked at Bob Rice's Weather Window based in New Hampshire in the US. The advice would help determine the most likely route Cabot would have taken given the conditions and circumstances the crew would face en route. With decades of experience the legendary Bob Rice was an institution for land, sea and air adventurers, having assisted dozens of high profile expeditions.

The modern navigation and communication equipment on board

THE MATTHEW

VOYAGE TO NEWFOUNDLAND

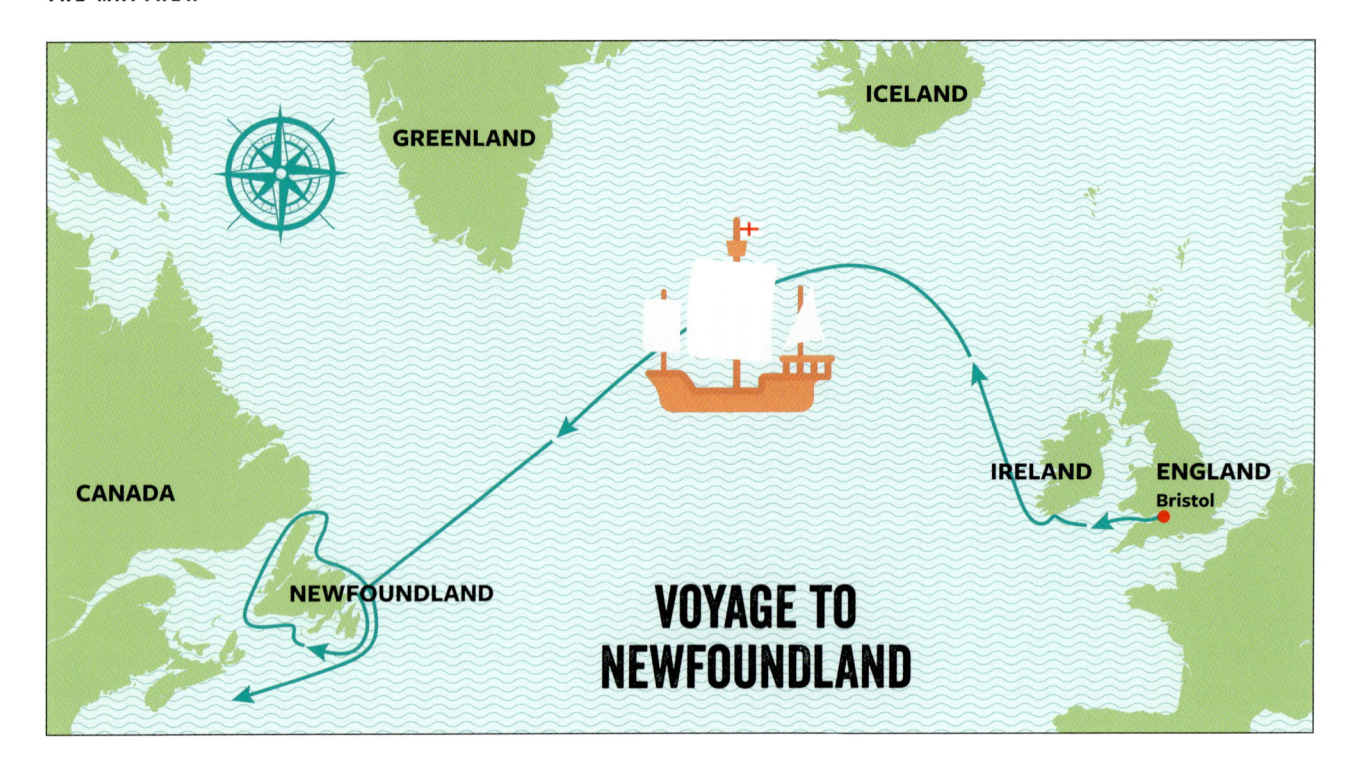

In addition to the satellite telecoms system, a SSB marine radio for long range communication, VHF radios, and a GSM mobile phone were also used to transmit and receive information. At 12 noon every day, the log recorded the exact position of the ship in latitude and longitude as well as the number of nautical miles travelled over 24 hours and the total miles sailed since departure. With BBC producer Steve Greenwood and cameraman Orlando Stuart on board as part of the crew, the eyes of the world were certainly on the *Matthew* as she made her way westwards. Their job was to cover the voyage for a series of six programmes on BBC1 – filming a continuous record of life on board, including the successes, the set-backs, the frustrations and the elation. And there would be plenty of those. The video material was transmitted by microwave link to a BBC team on board a Nimrod aircraft flown by 201 Squadron from RAF Kinloss on the Moray Firth in Scotland. The plane made regular contact with the ship and circled the vessel whilst the video footage was beamed-up. The first programme was due for transmission on May 25, 1997, and the last on June 25 – the day after arrival in Newfoundland, assuming the *Matthew* made it!

Away from the technology, the information overload and the continued attention from the media and well-wishers, the crew had a serious job to do – the re-enactment of Cabot's 1497 voyage across the North Atlantic.

The following edited extracts from the daily logs completed by the Captain provide a fascinating and compelling insight into what life was like on board over the next 54 days.

Off Portishead on May 4, 1997 – accompanied by a flotilla of craft

SHIP'S LOG by Captain David Alan-Williams

MAY 4 – By the time Clevedon is approached the tide is about to turn and with an unfavourable wind, there would be little chance of progress. So anchor is dropped in Clevedon Bay, just off the famous pier. It is a last stop at his home town for Mark Chislett, who used to be the coxswain of the local inshore rescue craft. David Redfern, the ship's publicity and press manager, goes ashore after hitching a ride to get home. Then Lawrence Freeman, from Cabot College and the ship's technical consultant, with his wife, Helen, come back in the Challenger RIB to say a final farewell. Now we are on our own. Kevin and Peter are first on the cooking roster today. After lunch, there is a buzz of activity as final preparations are made for going to sea, putting away stores. Then a calm quietness covers the ship as many crew catch up on sleep or recover, in James's case, from last night's party. With the tide turning fair in the early evening, anchor is raised at 7pm and after a single cannon is fired at Clevedon by Mark, The Matthew proceeds down the Bristol Channel.

MAY 5 – After being up in the crow's nest for a time to set and recover the Topsail, Chris and Peter are feeling less than stable on their feet and in the stomach for a while after. The forecast is for strong winds tonight of gale force 8 and 35-40 knots of wind. As a result we are heading for Milford Haven, to avoid being caught in the worst of the storm. Short of Milford Haven entrance the wind fills in with a rapid increase in sea state. There is no option but to stay outside and ride out the gale with some shelter under the cliffs.

THE MATTHEW

MAY 6 – *By day break it is a lost cause to seek shelter in Milford Haven. The sails are trimmed to head west to Ireland. After being rocked and rolled about for the last 20 hours a few items have come loose including a plaster cast Newfoundland dog given by the children of St Johns. During the afternoon there were various visits by RAF jets and a Fishery Protection plane. The course was initially good, but it swung back, so after three hours the ship is back in the same position.*

MAY 7 – *The cold wind has meant bringing out all the warm clothing and woolly jumpers. By morning the conditions are what being at sea are all about: sunshine between the clouds, fresh breeze of 20 knots, sails set and making 3.5 to 4.5 knots of speed. It is a good opportunity to complete many essential maintenance tasks – fixing rope loops, touching up the timbers with oil, working on the rigging and making canvass covers. The double-bang of Concorde was heard again as a reminder of last Saturday.*

MAY 8 – *By morning it was grey, overcast and damp with a big sea running. This made life a worry for Nick and Chris in the galley and after several spillages the galley is like an ice rink, so you can slide across the galley floor as the ship rolls. The aftermath of breakfast resembled a fall-out zone. The efforts to get to Ireland were looking low, until mid-morning when the sun came out, and the wind moderated. So now the tiller room looks like a laundry house with cloths and t-towels drying and the course is towards Waterford.*

MAY 9 – *In the Celtic Sea. It is days like the last 24 hours that make us appreciate the skills and patience of past seafarers, relying on the fickle whims of the wind to grace a sailing ship by blowing in a favourable direction. During the afternoon a violent rain squall lashed the ship, but there is always sunshine after rain and a school of common dolphins came alongside to play. It is the plan to make a stop in Ireland, to get last supplies of fresh food. But at present the wind gods are making it hard to get there. Maybe tomorrow…*

MAY 10 – *The daily routine is now well established with food and eating being the main focus. Despite misgivings of the pairing of James and Mark in the galley, nobody died overnight. Even compliments were heard about a combination of fresh and reconstituted dehydrated foods. A far cry from the food of Cabot's time, being salted fish and meats with dried fruit and lentil porridge mix. The present Matthew is a constant reminder of the contrast in life 500 years ago and now. Whilst Kevin and Peter are hand stitching to make canvas bags, rock & roll is blasting out of a stereo system. The sun is shining on the emerald fields of Ireland, and there is a thirst to share some local hospitality tonight for a brief stop in Crosshaven in Cork Harbour.*

MAY 11 – *On shore at Crosshaven.*

MAY 12 – *During our stopover, the renowned Irish hospitality came to the fore. Some of the crew were all but hijacked after meeting up with members of the local rugby club. It was not until ties, books and a shield had been exchanged with the President of the club that I, as captain, could get the crew back from enjoying the club's ambience and a diet of local ale. At 12-noon we left Crosshaven and after a wild exit out of Cork Harbour with a fresh wind and a steep sea the ship made good progress. It was only 90 miles to our final port of departure.*

MAY 13 – *Someone arriving on board ship at daybreak would have been confused as to where they were; in a bakery, a disco or a gym. Kevin was baking fresh bread with music at full volume and this was followed by Nigel's fitness class. As* the sun is out overhead, Jack is holding his navigation class showing Peter the use of the sextant. Seeing the wild beauty of the Southern Irish coastline, with harbours and bays behind prominent headlands, there is a general desire to come back again to explore at leisure.

MAY 14 – The menu on Fridays is fish, normally out of a tin if there is no fresh catch of the day. So the challenge is on to supply the 'catch of the day'. Martin produced a fluorescent green line in the belief that the fish would go for it at night and Russell T has ambitions on a 200 pound marlin judging from the size of his tackle. The fish around Matthew may survive some time yet. Now in Castletown Bearhaven, it is time for final preparations, buy stocks of fresh food and do jobs that take five minutes on a level keel in harbour rather than an hour at sea.

MAY 15 & 16 – In a small community like Castletown word got around fast that the Matthew was in port; the ship's history and the importance of this being the final departure point. There is a great sense of Irish pride to be able to help in some way with this historic voyage. A lot got done in the brief stopover and Michael of the local Spar food shop had a big smile after we cleared him out of fresh provisions; Brendan of the Fisherman's Co-operative organised the supply of diesel and Ian of the Bantry camera shop fixed up an underwater camera.

Leaving the shore team behind and with cannons firing for the last time this side of the Atlantic, at 13.30 Matthew took leave of Castletown Bearhaven. By 18.00 Dursey Head and Bull Rock had been passed and there is no more land in sight. Only the Atlantic is ahead. Now the voyage begins in earnest as we endeavour to establish the route that John Cabot took with his Matthew when he set out to find a trade route to Japan...

The crew giving the underside a fresh coat of white paint at Castletown Bearhaven

Russell Thiessen replacing the propellers

THE MATTHEW

MAY 17 – The engine starter motor failed when it was time to charge the batteries. The shore team of David Redfern and Laurel Alan-Williams are still in Castletown Bearhaven and Lawrence Freeman in Bristol. Despite being 07.30 on a Saturday morning, the plan was soon in place – source the replacement part in Ireland or Bristol then find a boat to come out to Matthew, 25 miles off Dingle Bay. By 10.30 Lawrence had collected a new caterpillar starter motor and Ron Bond is on his way with it from Bristol to catch the ferry from Fishguard to Rosslare and drive to Dingle. Laurel has established contact with Mike Denison in Dingle whose vessel 'Merlin Diver' is now on standby to come out with the part. David Redfern received great help from a caterpillar dealer in Cork, so a backup is on its way as well.

MAY 18 – The fishing competition resumed. Honours for the first catch of the day have gone to Martin as in the space of eight minutes as many mackerel were landed. Jack had them cleaned, gutted and filleted in no time ready for breakfast. At the first grey glimmer of daylight, the converted fishing trawler 'Merlin Diver' chugged out of the mist at 5 o'clock this morning. It is a welcome sight to see Ron Bond's grin having come from Bristol to this Atlantic rendezvous in under 20 hours, bringing the starter motor. No wonder the crew have nick-named him Agent Bond 007½. With Ron, Laurel and David Redfern as well as the crew of the 'Merlin Diver' aboard, it was only appropriate to take a nip from the barrel of brandy that the Matthew Society had presented before departure. The shore team had worked a small miracle. It is time to set sail again and to make what must be the final and seventh farewell departure as the sun climbs into the sky to burn away the mist.

MAY 19 – Sunday is to be a special day during the voyage, with the crew all sitting down to share a meal. Mark and James excelled themselves with the menu of roast beef wellington and Christmas puddings. Reverend Russell conducted a ceremony of grace followed by communion after the meal. Jack read out the correct lesson from St Mark's that he was meant to read at the church service on May 1, the starting day of the adventure. The dinner dress code for Sundays is either full medieval attire or jacket and tie. A stowaway pigeon and a very exhausted swallow have been taking a rest on board and Russell's pastoral services were further needed when the swallow died and was buried at sea.

The *Matthew* and the *Merlin Diver* in the background

MAY 20 – *The other side of the James Bond/Mission Impossible starter motor story has emerged. Imagine the scene at a small Irish port when a trawler suddenly gets ready for sea after not working for a time. First one, then a second English car turns up with the drivers making frantic mobile phone calls – trying not to be overheard whilst writing down positions. At 11pm another English car arrives at the quay. Boxes and tubes are quickly taken aboard the trawler which leaves into the mist. No wonder the Garda took an interest, got a retired customs man aboard and arranged another trawler to tag along. There were roars of laughter from the Dingle Harbourmaster when all was explained by the Matthew 'snatch squad' on return to port. It was the talk of the town – and David our PR man has not been seen since entering a welcoming Dingle pub. Meanwhile back at sea – steady progress at 2-3 knots – and a weekly hot shower was enjoyed by the crew.*

MAY 21 – *A typical 'Matthew Day'. There are no idle hands, no prisoners taken. Jack & Matthew produced the best version of Chunky Chicken so far; the Rev 'flags' Russell O is back to his mission of making a canvas bag for all 70+ flags on board; Mark and Gerry are on leak patrol; Orlando films and Steve is editing ready for Thursday's Nimrod fly-past; James & Kevin are making chafe pads for rigging and timber; Nigel is re-fixing down the anchors; Chris is always making up rope 'whatsits'; Luke is painting the emergency generator and Peter is making up a tackle system. We have officially left Europe now as the continental shelf fell away below our keel.*

MAY 22 – *Yesterday afternoon, the demolition team of Nigel & Nick set about the galley. When last filling the fresh water tanks, the starboard one under the galley floor got over pressured and bowed out and sprung the floorboard. Getting to the tank meant dismantling part of the galley units to lift all the boards. The floor boards lie flush again. On locating a leg of pork and finding*

VOYAGE TO NEWFOUNDLAND

Stowaway swallow and pigeon taking a rest on board

May 21, 1997 – a typical *Matthew* day and some fine sailing weather

Rev Russell Owen busily working on canvas bags to store the flags

the stocks of fresh vegetables are approaching their sell-by date, a gastronomic roast dinner was devoured by a hungry crew – washed down with a glass of ale medieval style.

MAY 23 – *It is a Matthew red letter day – a record daily run of 123.9 miles and passing 1,000 miles logged since Bristol. It is a great day of sailing – full sail set, sunshine at day, bright full moon at night, another brief appearance of a whale, also a swallow resting up as well as skuas and kittiwakes circling and a sucker fish attached to the hull. Just in case we thought we are the only people out here, there was human contact when the RAF Nimrod circled overhead for over an hour for the microwave uplink of the TV video footage.*

MAY 24 – *For a couple of hours around 50 long finned pilot whales played around the ship. It was Fuji film benefit day as lots of pictures were taken of the ocean where a whale had been the second before! Russell T continues to show his mechanical genius and Tasmanian resourcefulness as a love-hate relationship develops with the generator. Nigel continues his 'take it apart and fix it' role, with Kevin as partner this time to find a fuel leak dripping onto their bunks. The fault was found to be left over from the winter refit.*

MAY 25 – *It is now just another grey damp day with a fresh 20 knots south westerly breeze. In yesterday's drier conditions the main hold hatch was taken apart to hunt for leaks. As the ship ages, the timbers are moving, and what were once tight joints are now opening up just enough for water to get in. Sunday lunch is going to see the end of the fresh meat taken on in Ireland as the crew will all be eating together a menu of foods that would have been around in Cabot's day – beef, turnips, pea soup, jumbles (a knotted biscuit), cider and ale.*

MAY 26 – *Safety is the paramount focus for the voyage, so a full practice was done for abandoning ship. Nigel took everyone through the muster drill and Martin demonstrated the firefighting drill and use of extinguishers. Then the dingy was launched to understand the problems of launching and recovery at sea. With Luke and Mark on board, Nigel then dived into the sea when Matthew was brought back alongside the dingy to show the problems of getting a body back on board. From sailing under full sail to getting the man back on deck took less than 15 minutes. With a water temperature of 13C there is little time before hypothermia would set in. After everyone had tested their personal MOB beacon, it was time for the last of the fresh beef for a medieval lunch.*

MAY 27 – *There seems to be a general theme that the 20th century equipment suffers glitches, but the basic medieval configuration of hull, masts, sails and rigging work as they would have done 500 years ago. It almost feels like Cabot is with us, and that he appreciates how this fine replica of his ship sails. The modern stuff is something else. A man inspired to set off into the unknown to find a new trade route to Japan would be fascinated by the modern navigational and mechanical equipment installed in the name of modern safety regulations. Modern man is blasé about the supply of electric power, machinery, water, cooking gas etc. But at sea, keeping all these systems on the go is a major task compared to the operation of a caravel sailing ship. There is one thing in common with seafarers over the centuries – that is the awe of seeing a large whale almost the size of the ship nearby, as was the case this morning.*

MAY 28 – *Today we are all battened down in the toughest wind and sea conditions yet experienced by the ship. Feeling small and isolated in a big sea – the wind is a steady 40 knots with gusts to 47. With an 'all hands on deck' call, the bonnet and drabbler are taken off the main course and the operation of brailing up the sail, lowering the 500kg yard to the deck,* removing the bonnets, bundling up the sail, hoisting the yard, dropping the sail, sheeting in and clearing up the spaghetti of lines, takes an hour. Matthew and crew are riding out the storm. As the ship heaves, rolls and pitches, with waves breaking over the main deck, there is relief and praise for the way Colin Mudie's design is riding the sea and for the way the Bristol shipwrights built her. She is a stout ship and John Cabot would be pleased to command her, just as I am. With minimal sail set, we are riding out the Atlantic gale.

MAY 29 – Today marks the passing of the mid-way point from Ireland to Newfoundland and half time for the planned total voyage time. The first real blow of wind since setting out across the Atlantic has gone and both the ship and crew passed the test well. So it is back to routine life again with Mark, Chris, Peter, Paul and Gerry of starboard watch taking up the inter watch deck scrubbing competition. The deck now resembles a chess board as each watch scrubs the planks white opposite the dirtiest section of un-scrubbed deck belonging to the other watch.

MAY 30 - The 3 o'clock log entry of "All well @ watch change" was bound to tempt fate. The wind immediately gust to 28 knots so it was all hands back on deck to drop the main, leaving the fore sail set. The barometer went into freefall, dropping three millibars in an hour. With waves slamming against the port hull side, the main deck is awash. After the front passed over mid-morning, the sun came and the wind rapidly swung round to the SW, but is still blowing at 45 knots. In the same way as Cabot would have done, we are riding out the storm, protecting the ship from damage.

MAY 31 – If we thought it was going to be a brief gale like the last one, then wrong again. In the middle of the rising chaos of nature buffeting the brave little ship, the medical team was called into action as my thumb got split. Nick with the

Chris LeGrow hanging on during 'the first real blow of wind' on May 29, 1997

Hauling down a staysail halyard

assistance of Nigel performed the delicate task of putting in three stitches whilst the ship rolled back and forth 30 degrees. With 12 of the team up on the fore castle to get the forecourse down, the battle went on for 15 long minutes. At the same time three others were needed on the helm to control the ship in the face of 30 foot waves and speeds up to 9.4 knots. One large wave broke over the stern, burying the stern castle and blowing in one of the timber windows. With the wind a steady 45 to 55 knots and gusts over 60, the tops of waves were smoking as the wind blew them away. Cascades of water flowed across the deck, but Matthew stood her ground and calmly rode the waves with a calmness that reassured us all. Bob stood guard at the helm as the storm raged storm force 10 to 11. Exhausted, damp, quiet and with a new respect of the sea, the crew stirred to set the canvas again at the 7 o'clock breakfast watch change. It is time to dry out, with the clothes lines out. Progress is slow. We are further away from Bonavista than this time yesterday.

JUNE 1 – *No one can say that any two days are the same around here. One day we are wondering if the ship can survive the severe storm winds and mountainous seas. Then 24 hours later, Matthew is all but becalmed and enjoying sunshine to dry out. Looking more like a floating launderette than a ship on an historic voyage. The crew of Cabot's time would probably have had little more than the clothes they stood in and little in the way of bedding – sleeping on the deck or on top of the barrels in the hold. With three weeks and 800 miles in a direct line to get to Bonavista Bay area, we are rolling along. The challenge is out to be the first to see Newfoundland and the Chairman of Helical Bar has put up a Churchill crown coin for the first sighting of land.*

JUNE 2 – *After Sunday dinner it was eyes down for the serious business of the evening. The pub quiz. With questions set by David Redfern, it was a titan battle of the watches with Terry's*

Drying out after the storm on May 31, 1997

team coming back to claim a one point victory. After a day of thick mist, just before the Nimrod arrived, the cloud base lifted for some hazy sunshine – essential for line of sight contact between ship and plane for the microwave link. BBC engineer Peter Kemp is in the plane to collect the uplink and was joined by Laurel and Lawrence. It is good to have such direct contact with the world when we are just a little cork in the ocean. The visits of 201 Squadron from RAF Kinloss will be missed as we pass out of their operational range.

JUNE 3 - *To avenge the outcome of the pub quiz, port watch are following Jack's pace to scrub down the decks; Martin helped Nigel who was hanging over the stern to re-install the Jon Buoy*

Man-over-Board unit that was accidently set off a few days ago and James and Chris have recoated the mast below the crow's nest with oil. Peter and Luke had a relatively stable day in the galley and the watch captains avoided deck work by taking it in turns to dismantle Orlando's defunct camera.

JUNE 4 – Although there is potential for 10 hours to be spent in one's bunk, getting quality sleep is a problem with five hours being the longest period to get uninterrupted sleep. The main daily menu is based around McDougall's dehydrated food, supplemented with tinned meats, rice, pasta, lots of condiment additives and chocolates. In a small ship bugs and colds spread quickly. There was a 24-hour head cold that did the rounds earlier and now it is a stomach virus setting off a violent chain reaction. The overload of use on the ship's two heads has produced inevitable blockages. The wind direction continues to shine on us as we are entering the third and final stage of the voyage – crossing iceberg country off the Grand Banks.

JUNE 5 – Just when you think you are away from everyone, company turns up. First contact was made yesterday afternoon with Canada in the form of an Orion patrol aircraft from the Canadian Air Force. The good news was their report of no icebergs for 100 miles ahead. At tea time the balloons and streamers were hanging, candles lit on the cake iced with a picture of Matthew by my father and an email message came in on the Stratos system from Orlando's mother – whose birthday was celebrated.

JUNE 6 – We may be out in the middle of the ocean but some items of news always travels. As a result of the Ashes cricket news from Edgbaston, the two crew from Down Under are considering changing nationality. The good fair winds have come to an end and during the night Matthew trickled to a halt, rolling gently most of the time with sails flapping. The cool air

One of several beautiful sunsets on the journey

is freeze drying everything. So, it is a normal Matthew day at sea. With Bob at the helm it is a matter of waiting for the breeze and push into iceberg territory next week.

JUNE 7 – Apart from the continuing sanding, oiling, hammering, rigging and canvas work, the biggest action round here is the abundance of wildlife. A school of pilot whales has been making regular visits for the last three days, sometimes accompanied by dolphins. A white bibbed seal named 'Sammy Seal' stares with shiny eyes at this strange apparition in his waters. The birds circle around looking intently at all aspects of the ship.

JUNE 8 – The elements are keeping Matthew en route for the full duration with a lack of wind to fill the sails. We are in a warmer spot out here in the ocean despite being further north than Bonavista. This convinced Paul then Peter and finally Chris to go for a dip in the bracing 13 degrees water temperature. For a couple of minutes, they were the fastest moving objects on the water, ahead of the convention of Fulmars paddling around the ship.

THE MATTHEW

A crew member's cramped bunk containing all of his worldly possessions!

The storage of food and provisions in weekly baskets

JUNE 9 – *Sunday is the red letter 'S' day – shower, shave and scrub down. A number of crew have given up the shaving habit for the voyage, so there is a great range of bush from Jack's well established growth to the stubble look of James and Peter. Kevin's birthday, completion of the main bulk of the Atlantic crossing and arriving at the official border of ice country are good cause to decorate the saloon with balloons and streamers for the Sunday medieval crew dinner. After a burst of song and with the party over, the wind filled in on cue from the North West. There is a great feeling of being on our way again to complete the task of following John Cabot's voyage.*

JUNE 10 – *The sun made an appearance today giving the navigation school a session. Peter and Terry had a shot at using the Astrolabe, which is an instrument John Cabot would have used to determine his latitude, north/south position. Compared to the GPS position of 50 deg 42 min north, Terry got 51 02N and Peter hoping for warmer climes got 47 02N, ie on the south side of Newfoundland. On a heaving rolling ship they are notoriously inaccurate. Meanwhile Jack was shooting the sun with a sextant to arrive within a mile or so of agreeing with the satellites above from which the GPS system works.*

JUNE 11 – *A gathering of the Bristol families at Luke's parents' house received a surprise call from the ship. It was like student accommodation to see how many people can get into the phone box of the port deck cabin. The seas are all now kicked up into sharp peaks, causing the ship to roll about more violently than usual. Despite the best efforts of Peter and Luke, this morning's breakfast was a disaster zone. Via an email from the Clevedon Mercury, Mark was informed that he is about to become an uncle and after hearing Jack's wild dream sequences, the port watch emerged on deck like scared lemmings.*

JUNE 12 – *Food is the focus of daily life with the three times* a day ritual of trying to get the contents of the plate into the target. This is done whilst bracing oneself around the table, holding onto the plate and cup, catching other items on the table as they fly by. The monotony of a weekly diet is telling. Stocks of apples, oranges, lemons, potatoes cheese and cabbages should last another week. Otherwise it is tinned or dried fruits. Although everyone craves for fresh steak, salad and milk, no one is looking thinner and the menu is a luxury compared to Cabot's day.

JUNE 13 – This morning has been one of the pleasantest days sailing of the voyage. The sun is shining bright, a moderate 15 knot breeze is pushing Matthew along, and there is little violent rolling motion. The only downside is the sharp drop in temperature with a chilling Arctic wind. There was a chance meeting of old meeting old. We passed the m/v Amstel bound for Reykjavik with a cargo of a Viking ship. They plan to row/sail it from Iceland to Greenland, Newfoundland and Nova Scotia this summer to cash-in on the Cabot 500 events. This was the first close physical contact at surface level with the rest of the world since leaving Dingle Bay. One interesting twist was that Matthew slipped under the Amstel's radar system and they spotted us by eye first. The worry is that it shows how ineffective the boat type radar reflectors are as we carry one aloft. The ship's artist, or more correctly cartoonist, has emerged to be Orlando, with an assassin's eye caricature sketch of every crew

member, in the alternative log. Definitely not something for publication without legal writs flying.

JUNE 14 – As Matthew approaches the 200 mile limit of Canadian offshore control, the countdown for arrival has started. This was highlighted by the second visit of the Canadian Coast Guard Fishery Patrol plane for the weekly video uplink. The aircraft gave us a flying display before heading off. With the full three square sails set, we are slipping along again at four knots. But the fine weather was yesterday's summer, now we have typical Grand Banks conditions; rain, drizzle, damp fog and from a quarter to half mile visibility. It is a morning for short stints on the whip staff on the stern castle, then find a job below.

JUNE 15 – "It's good caplin weather," says Jack. Cod feed on the caplin (or capelin) and man feeds on the cod. Or at least used to on the Grand Banks. The stories from Cabot's voyage were that every basket lowered overboard would fill with 'stock fish'. It is commonly believed that the Bristol fishermen were catching fish on the Grand Banks as much as 20 to 30 years before Cabot's voyage. In similar weather conditions to now it would be possible that those fishermen never saw land. The east coast of Newfoundland would have appeared very bleak then as it does now. The grey damp mist rolls back 'n forth, sometimes there is 200 metres visibility, occasionally as much as a couple of miles. The big swell of the North Atlantic has gone to be replaced by short steep waves. It may be just a short run in to the finish line with time in hand, but it could be as big a test of sailing skills as any part of the voyage.

JUNE 16 – Every day is different. At one point in the afternoon we meandered along in the fog with the sun out overhead whilst it rained and the wind blew 24 knots from the south west as the north west swell rocked the ship irregularly. Work that one out.

Overnight the fog cleared, the stars were seen for the first time in many days as well as the moon. Then a bitingly cold north west breeze filled in. The water temperature has dipped below four degrees and the air is not much warmer. The stern castle deck became treacherous as Steve found out when he slid across it crashing into Paul, knocking the contents of his cup over Peter, with everyone ending up on their backsides including Mark at the helm from laughter! With the sun out and sails set, Gerry is doing an imitation of a koala bear up the mizzen mast; Chris is on the rigging; Terry is head down sorting the shower pump; Russell O is considering a new career as a sailmaker and Matthew and Jack are the first to sign-off for their last time on galley duty.

JUNE 17 – Making use of the sunshine and moderate breeze, the starboard watch carries on with deck maintenance tasks. The first signs of approaching land are appearing. These are not of the type that Cabot would have looked for, such as land birds, driftwood and seaweed. Rather it is fishing floats and fishing boats, and the local Newfoundland radio stations. Fishermen the world over look but don't speak first, so it was ships passing on the ocean. The brashness and clutter of commercial radio with its less than subtle adverts is a sharp contrast to the natural open space of life at sea. 'Matthew' fever is building ashore by the tones of the DJs though a variety of different times have been given for the arrival at Bonavista in a week's time.

JUNE 18 – The fine sunny weather lasted through to the final video link to the Canadian Fishery Patrol plane. With the wind up to 25 knots Matthew is flying along with spritsail, mainsail and lateen sails set. Sailing at four knots with the wind angle 70 degrees off the bow, it is some of the best sailing of the voyage. It was too much to ask for fine weather lasting more than a day or so. The fog, drizzle and mist rolled back in over our little ship this morning. This last stage of the voyage is proving to be as difficult as any part as the wind comes and goes, fluctuates in direction but is always coming from where we want to go. The distance to go is glued to 120 miles. It is wriggle, wriggle, and wriggle to keep the ship sailing. The other worry came after listening to the Coast Guard weather and warnings broadcast. Bonavista Harbour is shut to visiting vessels from June 21. I hope they let us in.

JUNE 19 - The all-embracing fog blankets out any sign of the horizon. No wonder strange tales arise from the minds of crews on ships drifting in fog. There was a strong smell of rotting seaweed most of the night, as if it could have been from the stale breath of whales around us. Before the wind went completely, it suddenly dropped to nothing for a few minutes and just as quickly returned as if we had passed the wind shadow of something large like an iceberg. Nothing was seen or detected by eye or radar. With the wind down, the ship gently rolled to a constant rhythm. But then with no cause she rolled violently from side to side, as occurs from the wake of a large ship passing by at speed. After reaching 100 miles to Bonavista, we drifted back five miles north. So close and yet so far.

JUNE 20 – At the 2300 watch change, as the wind is now blowing a steady 30 knots, the main sail and yard are lowered and stowed by all hands on deck. With a short, sharp sea building, the waves lunge out of the mist and smack into the hull side. The ship shakes and shudders in some of the most stressful conditions she has had to endure. The radar is monitored as a couple of targets are observed which pass by and are assumed to be fishing boats. Past sailors must have lived off their nerves in such conditions without modern technology to know their position or have radar eyes to penetrate the mirk. As the fog begins to roll back, letting in the sun, Mark calls, "Iceberg!" He has consistently been the first to spot whales and anything else of note. Within minutes the fog clears back to the horizon,

The first iceberg – spotted by Mark Chislett

the sun is bright and the blue/green hue of the berg reflects in the light. Out come the cameras. "Are we going to take a close look?" says Peter. Why not. As we approach there are a lot of small bergy bits and growlers, keeping us a quarter of a mile away. The tender is launched with Mark, Luke and Orlando and a shop full of cameras to film the ship sail by and take a closer look. The first berg of the voyage and the first for most of the crew. As we wear ship to head south, another bigger berg is spotted down track on the course we had been sailing in the fog. What would Cabot have thought at such a sight? Certainly there would have been fascination and a high degree of concern for his ship's safety. Some things don't change in 500 years. But to get a phone call in the open sea is something he wouldn't have experienced. There is a buzz of excitement ashore. The news from David Redfern is that the flotilla fleet coming down the St Lawrence has arrived in St John's. The 80 yachts will move to Bonavista for the weekend and meet us there.

THE MATTHEW

Crew members concentrating hard on tasks during one of the watches

JUNE 21 – The iceberg siting has turned into a good omen for the weather, with clear sunny skies. With the sun and moon in aspect, the sun's light was replaced with a shimmering moonlit night. This helped with the iceberg watch on the forecastle deck. The practical limit is 20 minutes before one's eyes start playing tricks that every little wave is a bergy bit. The big icebergs only show up on radar within five miles and are spotted by eye first with no fog around. The small pieces, which are still capable of puncturing the timber planks are only visible by eye. Russell O's turn on duty ended when he shouted out "Iceberg" only to be told by the rest of the watch that it was the white superstructure of the Canadian Coast Guard ice patrol ship Leonard J Cowley that had been observed 15 minutes before! The Channel Fever syndrome is building as there are multiple wild claims of seeing land to claim the Churchill crown, but it was just an iceberg against the fog bank.

JUNE 22 – Takemukek (the Micmac Indian tribe's name for Newfoundland) was first sighted at 1315 GMT, by Mark and Russell O at the same time, whilst looking at some distant icebergs, to claim the crown. It was identified as Fogo Island – the first land seen for 37 days since clearing Dursey Head in Ireland. This morning the starboard watch are a bunch of bilge rats as all the floor boards came up on deck for cleaning. Being a man of God, Sunday is a day of prayer and thought for Russell O. His Archdeacon has praised his television appearances for helping awareness of the church. But there were certain doubts amongst the rest of the bilge rat squad that he was communing with the above when he was noted standing up to his ankles in bilge water with his eyes firmly shut. Only to come to with a start when dropping the scrubbing brush onto his foot. Was it Holy thought, blanking out the nightmare of the bilges or getting in a quick 40 winks of sleep, Russell? As we get closer to shore, the paddle presented by Chief Mi'sel Joe of the Micmac Indian tribe when we were at Redcliffe Wharf shortly before departure, was signed by all the crew. When we arrive in Newfoundland, the paddle will be returned and it will be used to paddle a canoe across Cabot Straight to link the Micmac Tribe's settlements in Newfoundland and Nova Scotia – the two most likely lands that Cabot coasted along on his voyage.

The Canadian Coast Guard ship, the Leonard J Cowley *welcomes the* Matthew *into Canadian waters. Chris LeGrow keeps watch*

VOYAGE TO NEWFOUNDLAND

Sunday June 22, 1997. The last supper and the crew are treated to Chris LeGrow's Aunt Effie's homemade cookies!

JUNE 23 – Sunday's medieval dinner was the last time the crew all sat to share food together. The last supper. Also it was good reason to celebrate, for the voyage is all but over, with just a day to go. The Leonard J Cowley came back and must have been confused by the scene of a medieval caravel drifting about with all sails scandalised; no one visible on deck and Irish jig music blasting out from below. Their curiosity got the better of them and after sending up their helicopter initially to check out the area, then their RIB to circle around and finally the ship all but came alongside, the Matthew crew emerged from dinner in full period clothing. There was an exchange of mutual photograph taking, but invitations on this occasion were for members of the Atlantic Medieval Club only.

With land sighted and just over 35 miles to the landfall site, how does this voyage compare with Cabot's 500 years ago? With the records indicating that he took just 15 days for the return passage, is it realistic that it took more than 50 days to reach Newfoundland? Despite being driven backwards 50 miles in a couple of storms, it looked at one stage we would be two weeks ahead of Cabot. But the last 500 miles have been anything but straightforward. The wind has twisted and turned to be on the nose with very little free wind sailing. Combined with it changing daily from calm to 25 knots in strength, then thick fog, and being cautious for icebergs, it has been a testing final stage.

The sextant, astrolabe, rope log and observations of sun and stars have been made in the traditional manner. Certainly using the instruments of Cabot's time, it is a miracle they ever knew where they were in comparison to the pin-point accuracy of GPS and radar navigation. Although we have received weather faxes and ice reports advice, at the end of the day we have sailed where the wind has taken us. A question often asked is, are we cheating by motoring to keep to the timeline? Basically no. When running the water maker from the main engine, the gears are engaged at minimum rev, in order to load the diesel engine so it does not glaze over. This has benefitted us no more than 150 miles out of the 2,850 miles sailed. Without the benefit of an original log book, we will never know the route of Cabot's Matthew 500 years ago. But given the conditions we have encountered and given the ship which is as close a sister to the original, John Cabot could have sailed a similar course to ours if he was doing it again this year.

With the voyage almost done and 24-hours before arrival, it was a time for reflection and the four Canadian crew recorded their thoughts:

John Jack Smith: *"Our arrival in Bonavista tomorrow will be a historic event for England, all of Canada and North America in the re-enactment of John Cabot's arrival to our shores 500 years ago. While crossing the Grand Banks the water was teeming with cod fish so much so it slowed his ship. His discovery of Newfoundland and the abundance of cod fish encouraged English, Irish and Europeans to emigrate to harvest the cod. For me this event is very special in many ways. First that I was chosen at my age to make this voyage. I consider Cabot's arrival in Newfoundland as an ancestral part of my family heritage as both of my grandfathers were of English and Irish stock. They emigrated in the early 1800s and married my Newfoundland grandmothers, also of English stock. Both had large families who continued to harvest the cod for a living. My father was a very successful fishing skipper known as the Fish Killer, referred to in local books and along the Eastern Seaboard. I also fished the Grand Banks 62 years ago, which developed into my sea-going career and provided me with a comfortable living. I was very happy to be fortunate enough to make this voyage due to my connection with ships and the sea. I am very proud of my ancestral heritage and to be born Newfoundland Canadian. Thanks for the opportunity."*

Chris LeGrow: *"This voyage of discovery and adventure means many different things to the crew on board. Bonavista, Canada, being the final destination makes the arrival extra special for me as it is my home I am returning to. I am one of many Newfoundlanders that see this voyage as a way to re-live our rich history and to use it as a milestone in bettering ourselves for the 21st century. It is also another excuse for a year-long kitchen party."*

Peter Zimonjic: *"Arriving in Bonavista will be like coming full circle. Re-enacting a voyage that led to the forming of Canada, a country where my parents met, fell in love and decided to raise a family. Without Canada I wouldn't be. Completing the journey also fulfils the need in all of us, big or small, for adventure and challenge in our lives. I am grateful we have had the opportunity we did."*

Luke Porter: *"When we left Bristol seven weeks ago many of the crew looked back at the homes they left. I looked forward to the home I was sailing to. As we got closer to Bonavista things became more familiar, the sea, the weather, the radio stations. The arrival of the Matthew finally connects the place I was born, Bristol, with the place I live, Newfoundland, in a unique and exciting way. What are the odds of a project like this occurring in my lifetime – this realisation of a connection? The completion of the voyage will be a huge moment in my life no matter what else happens."*

Just outside Bonavista on Tuesday, June 24, 1997, and 54 days and 2,881.9 miles since leaving Bristol, the crew was busy making final preparations to make landfall as Cabot

The *Matthew*, just off the coast of Bonavista

Sails now stowed, the *Matthew* just outside the harbour

had done 500 years earlier. The re-enactment of the historic voyage was coming to an end. With the *Matthew* bedecked in flags and the crew looking splendid in their medieval costumes it was time for the skipper's final 12-noon entry:

JUNE 24 – "*500 years ago today the Italian Giovanni Caboto landed on what he called New Founde Lande. Barely recorded at the time and all but ignored by the history books, this event was the start of many events.*

It was the first official voyage from the English nation overseas for the purpose of exploring the possibility of new trade routes to the Far East. It marked the start of English settlements in North America. It could be considered to be the start of the spread of British influence and subsequent power internationally. Without Cabot's tentative, though successful, voyage of exploration and the subsequent English expeditions, the new nations of Canada and the United States could have French, Portuguese or Spanish as the primary language.

It is more than just a coincidence that in a week's time Hong Kong is being relinquished from British control. This could be taken to mark the completion of the cycle of Britain as an international super power. In that respect it is appropriate for the Queen to join the celebration of Cabot's landfall today at Bonavista for an event that is a milestone in history.

As we approach the harbour for the celebrations this afternoon, there is an end of term feeling about the ship. Bags are being finished off to pack up clothes and gear for the off-loading. The watch system has ended. After a day of calm and fog, the new breeze from the north west cleared the fog and the rain. The sails are set as Matthew approaches the final safe haven of this voyage. The big lady is about to take the stage for the very last song.

Having been living in our own little world these last few weeks, that lifestyle is about to change. The priority for us is to be with families again. There are a number of surprises for some of the crew as it has been a secret that their wives, partners, friends and families are turning up. We have heard the local radio channels reporting and the TV and media are there on the quay. It is a grey bleak day and after the rain cleared in the morning a fresh south west wind has set in to blow Matthew on the final stage of the voyage."

The day after arrival. A sunny morning greets the *Matthew* in Bonavista Harbour

HELLO NEWFOUNDLAND AND LABRADOR

If the farewell from Bristol with all of its pomp and ceremony was spectacular, the welcome in Newfoundland was extraordinary.

For Newfoundlanders and Labradorians, this was their 500th anniversary too and 1997 was a year-long, province-wide celebration with a series of festivals and hundreds of community events to mark Cabot's voyage and the resulting European settlement of the New World. Billed as the biggest event in the history of the province tens of thousands of tourists poured into the area. Visitor guides helpfully divided the celebrations and events into the region of Labrador and the four regions of Newfoundland – Western, Central, Eastern and Avalon. A massive boost for tourism and the struggling coastal economy, the umbrella organisation, 'The John Cabot (1997) 500th Anniversary Corporation', with its specially designed logo, oversaw six so called 'Anchor Events':

- **Festival 500 Sharing the Voices**. Across 11 days, adult and youth choirs from ten countries performed at various venues and a gala-concluding concert featured a 400-voice youth choir and a 400-voice adult choir accompanied by a 100-piece Festival Orchestra.
- **Cabot and His World Symposium**. A six-day event that brought together local, national and international scholars and authorities to debate Cabot's voyages and the lasting impact of European arrival in Eastern North America. Genealogists also ran workshops exploring family links between Newfoundland and the West of England.
- **The Northern Lights Celebrations**. Two weeks of winter sporting and cultural events; competitive Nordic skiing; drama; native arts and crafts and the Labrador 400 International Sled Dog Race.
- **Year of the Arts 1997**. Billed as a 'Canadian first', more than 1,300 dancers, sculptors, writers, musicians, poets, painters and cinematographers joined together in a festival to celebrate the thriving arts community in the province – and participated in more than 75 unique events.
- **The Summit of the Sea**. With the coastal communities in Newfoundland and Labrador in crisis owing to a moratorium on fishing, the opportunity was taken to host an international conference in St John's. More than 3,000 policy makers from around the world attended to discuss the sustainable use of the ocean's resources – the largest conference of its type in the world during 1997 and a forerunner to the 1998 United Nations Year of the Oceans.
- **The *Matthew* Visit**. The highlight of the year of celebration was of course the arrival of the *Matthew* on June 24, 1997, and the re-enactment of the landfall exactly 500 years earlier.

THE MATTHEW

Mark Chislett preparing to charge the cannon as the Matthew gets closer to land

Almost there. Family, friends, the media and dignitaries about to welcome the Matthew and her crew.

CELEBRATING THE ARRIVAL

During the following 46 days, the little ship would visit 17 ports in an itinerary developed by a Matthew Marine Advisory sub-committee. Each of the 17 settlements had their own local committee to co-ordinate the celebratory events and to welcome the *Matthew* as it circumnavigated the island.

The longest ever live broadcast in the history of Canadian broadcasting showed the arrival coast to coast. BBC news and documentary crews, including presenter Peter Snow, were on hand to record proceedings, and so were Richard Wyatt the local news anchor for HTV television in Bristol and David Harrison from the Bristol Evening Post. The international media were there in force and television networks broadcast one of the greatest spectacles in Canadian history.

As the *Matthew* made its way to the harbour it was greeted by 'Newfoundland Flotilla 97' – a spectacular gathering of more than 100 yachts ranging from a 21 foot Finesse Sloop to a 110 foot Brigantine. The first yachts departed Toronto Harbour six weeks earlier and more joined en-route through the Great Lakes and the St Lawrence as the flotilla made its way south. Many of the vessels would accompany the *Matthew* on its passage around Newfoundland.

Before that though, there were emotional scenes on the quayside at Bonavista as the *Matthew* came alongside at three o'clock and members of the crew caught sight of family, friends and loved-ones for the first time in 53 days and who had flown in secretly to meet them. Most of the Matthew Project team including Chairman St John Hartnell and financial backer Michael Slade had also flown in especially as did many members of the Matthew Society.

One notable absentee was Martyn Heighton. He'd recently taken up the position of Chief Executive of the *Mary Rose* Trust and was unable to see his original idea through to its end, "…on the morning I should have been in Bonavista, I was addressing my first meeting of the *Mary Rose* Trustees", he once lamented. Back in Bristol, other Matthew Society volunteers toasted the arrival with a celebratory glass or two of champagne. At Cabot Tower on Brandon Hill, Bristol, a group of amateur radio enthusiasts made contact with their opposite numbers who had set up a temporary shortwave

Family members with a 'Well Done' flag wait to greet loved ones

The Landfall Celebration Dancers entertaining the crowd

Martin Pick, David and Laurel Alan-Williams and... The Queen

John Jack Smith, the oldest crew member engulfed by the media

radio station at Newfoundland's own Cabot Tower on Signal Hill, overlooking the narrow entrance to St. John's harbour.

Back at Bonavista Harbour, the provincial, national and international media were jostling for the best arrival photographs and exclusive crew interviews, but this was put on hold for a while as it was time for the Matthew Landfall Ceremony to get fully underway. The dockside was transformed for the occasion. Already entertained by choirs and performers the audience of 3,200 wrapped up warm to brave chill winds, a grey sky and freezing temperatures. Immediately in front of the *Matthew* was a landfall re-enactment area; there were stages for performers, choirs and presenters and there was a Royal Box for the Queen and the project patron the Duke of Edinburgh. Other dignitaries included John Bruton, the Taoiseach of Ireland, Brian Tobin, the Premier of Newfoundland and Labrador, Sandra Kelly,

THE MATTHEW

CIRCUMNAVIGATING NEWFOUNDLAND

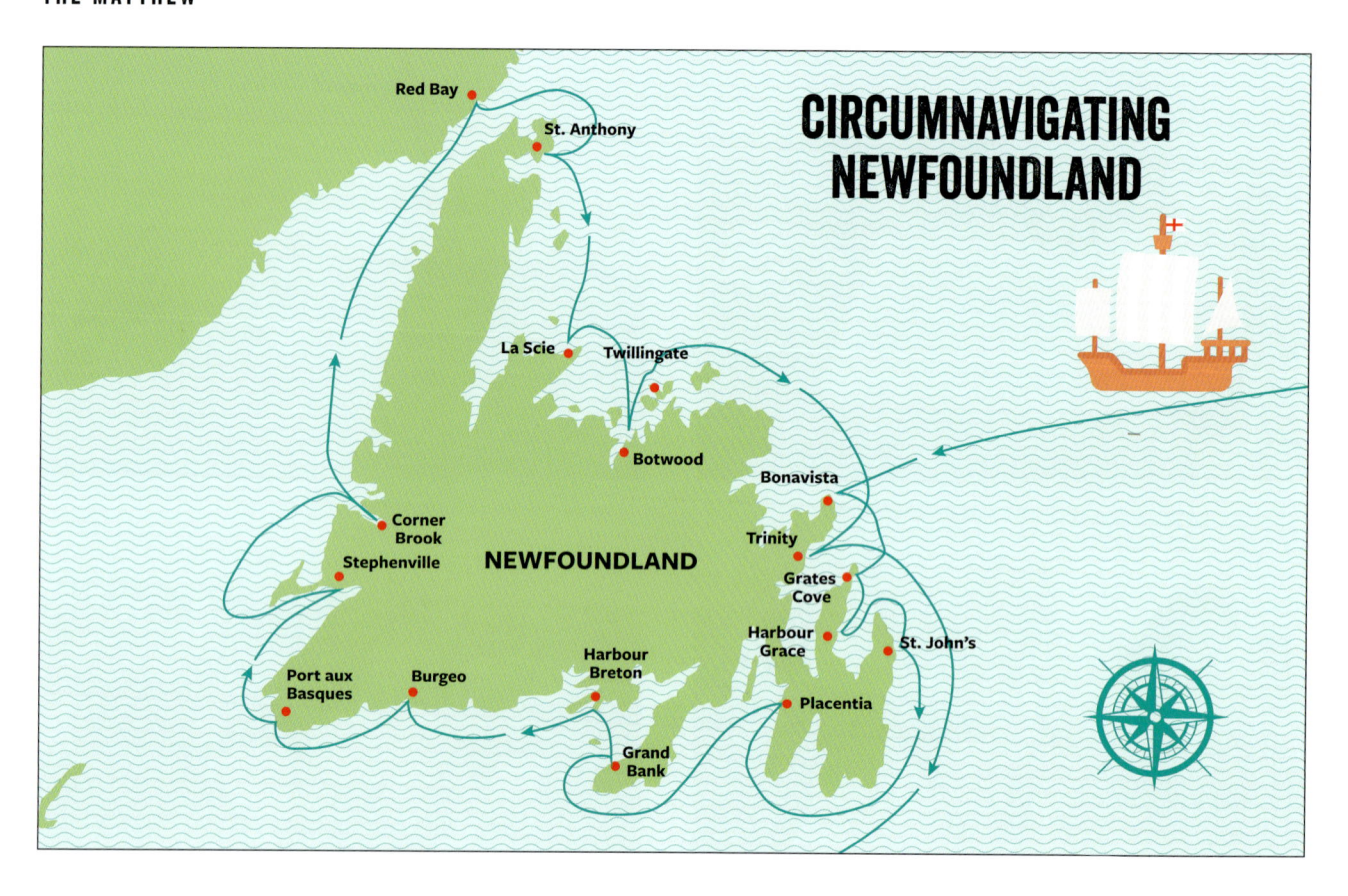

Newfoundland's Minister of Tourism, Culture and Recreation and Dr Franco Bozzolin an Italian Government Minister from Venice.

Master of Ceremonies was Gordon Pinsent a Newfoundland-born actor, screenwriter and playwright. His 24-page script was timed to the second. Starting at 12.45pm when the gates opened, it concluded at 16.45pm. In between, the musical accompaniment came from the Filton Choir from Bristol and local offerings from Newman Cove Choir, the Bonavista Celebration Choir, the Cabot Quintet Medley, the Folk of the Sea and the Irish Descendants. The historical re-enactment was performed by the Rising Tide Theatre Company and traditional Newfoundland dances were performed by the Landfall Celebration Dancers.

Her Majesty and David Alan-Williams were among the many who gave brief presentations to the assembled guests and to the media, and before the Royal party left, the Queen, Prince Philip and Brian Tobin were introduced to the crew.

There was little respite as the *Matthew* was available for public viewing in the evening and the day of celebration ended with waterfront fireworks at 10pm. On the following two days, the *Matthew* was open for viewing at the Bonavista dockside from 10am to 6pm before it departed on its tour around the island. Unlike the weather for its arrival,

Thousands flock to see the Matthew as she circumnavigates Newfoundland

Bonavista was bathed in sunshine for the next few days and viewed from on high, the *Matthew* looked magnificent in the harbour.

There were emotional goodbyes for most of the crew that had crossed the Atlantic. When the Bristol contingent arrived home they were greeted like heroes. Each received the Lord Mayor's Medal awarded for service to the city and Mark Chislett was whisked off to the Royal Oak in Clevedon where a BBC Points West team was waiting to interview him. The pub became a favourite watering hole for the crew before the adventure and still retains an area dedicated to all things Matthew. Here you can find pieces of oak left over from her construction – put to good use as a bar shelf – and another piece cleverly painted with a mural of the 1997 crew.

Meanwhile, back in Bonavista, David Alan-Williams and the remaining crew of Terry Nash, Russell Thiessen, James Roy, and John Jack Smith were joined for the 46-day, 17-port tour by temporary local crew and by Laurel Alan-Williams and David Redfern (the artist of the Royal Oak mural). There was a schedule and a calendar but none of the written information could have prepared the crew for the depth of feeling for the ship and the sheer scale of the numbers of people who were to visit. It was an adventure

Greenspond - An un-scheduled visit

Greenspond – Another enthusiastic welcome

Arrival at Grand Bank

that made crossing the North Atlantic seem calm in retrospect!

In an account written in September 1997, David Redfern takes up the story:

"The Government of Newfoundland and Labrador had put an enormous amount of money and effort into the arrival and the tour. We in Bristol had of course given the ship a tremendous send-off in May and the other side were determined not to be outshone. Every facility that was needed was available. We had an escort for the journey by a Canadian Coast Guard cutter, the *Grosswater Bay*, a Royal Canadian Mounted Police high speed catamaran, the *Simonds* and a road crew onshore of more than 100 people. It was like touring as a rock band and royalty combined.

At each port, the road crew had gone ahead and set up a giant mobile stage with deafening speakers systems, podiums for the speakers, exhibition marquees, sponsors' hospitality pavilions and dozens of concession stalls for local traders to sell their Matthew souvenirs and food.

Sometimes the logistics were horrendous. The *Matthew* would sail for 36 hours or so, but the road crew would have had 12-14 hours on the road to get to the next port and set up with two to three hours sleep in between. The ship was not let off either. The programme was so intense that we had to keep a watch on ourselves in port during the official ceremonies to avoid falling asleep. If one was on the 3am watch, finishing at 6am, then having breakfast, there would be no sleep because by 7am, all crew had to muster to get the ship ready for a typical 10am arrival. This meant deck scrubbing, sail hoisting, getting into costume and then getting ready for the routine that was to become very familiar by the end of the 46-day tour.

Arrival would see, first of all, small dory boats coming out to meet us often at 5am in the morning. These tiny boats had 90 horsepower engines and seemed to have the entire village in them including dogs!

As we got close to each port, every boat that would float came to greet us. Regularly this would be 60 boats – sometimes 100. The most was 145, every one packed to the hilt with people waving and cheering. It never failed to bring a lump to the throat to see the sheer love and affection for the *Matthew* by an island people who for seven years have had nothing but depression, misery and no jobs due to the fishing moratorium that has practically destroyed the economy of the province. We would visit villages or islands where no one was employed, where the only industry – fishing and the processing factories were dead. We began to understand the powerful feeling only after the first week, and we began to understand how important the visit of the *Matthew* was as a morale booster.

Local voluntary committees had worked together in a binding spirit for two years or more planning the local programme for the *Matthew*. It was difficult at times having had two or three hours sleep a day for two days before arriving as well as training the new crew on each leg and doing very physical work to fully take in the goodwill of the planned programmes.

David Alan-Williams and our crew would be cheered, with lines of people touching us and shaking hands. Children with eyes wide open at the sight of a bedraggled crew in medieval costume would think we were pirates as we staggered ashore to cheers from thousands of people on the quay sides.

Usually the first item on the agenda was a performance by the Rising Tide Theatre that was a 'landfall re-enactment ceremony'. The words and songs became engraved in our minds before too long, and we soon learnt to wait

THE MATTHEW

The Newfoundland flag flew with pride everywhere the Matthew went

Another quayside, another crowd of enthusiastic visitors

offshore until the end of the 40-minute show. Next would be a welcome from the local mayor and then the local committee. Usually there would be a church service ranging in time from a few minutes to almost an hour. In the French communities the ceremony would be in two languages.

On each leg of the journey, as well as volunteer crew, we had at least one Member of the House of Assemblies, perhaps a Minister and Members of the Federal Parliament. They would then give their impressions of the journey. This would be followed by an appraisal of the roles of the three sponsors, Labatt's Beer, Sobeys Supermarket and the Atlantic Marine Shipping Line. The sponsors would reply with their own speeches which were beginning to get known by heart by the crew.

Local musicians usually had written a song or two especially for the occasion, often 15 verses. Then we would have a preview of the evening concert by a tremendous group of boys called the 'Irish Descendants'.

After the ceremonies, with usually 11 speeches (the record was 18) the crew would be looking for a shower and change of clothes, often in a school a mile or so away. Most of the time the crew stayed on board the ship which was open to the public from 10am to 10pm. During this time, different crew members would be on engagements. It might be a lunch and talk at Rotary, a meal at the Lions Club for another crew, a tree-planting ceremony for the skipper, and then dinner and more speeches at night frequently with a play, a concert and more speeches until 1am or later.

Aboard ship, 3,000 people a day would do a trip around the deck with several of them coming below by mistake whilst we were changing clothes or having a sleep. At night the bands would play up to 1am, and we would also have on board the new crew for the next leg of the voyage who, of course, were very excited and curious to know every detail of the journey over and naturally, how to sail the ship. There were times when we were exhausted to a state of collapse, and yet of course, we kept smiling and kept the *Matthew* show on the road. The total population of the province of Newfoundland is 500,000 and it was estimated that 400,000 people came to see the *Matthew* and 60,000 came on board.

Each town we visited had its own special character and a reflection of its past origins. We would visit French ports, Basque towns, Irish areas and English West Country villages.

HELLO NEWFOUNDLAND AND LABRADOR

Almost the first greeting on arrival was a fisherman asking, "Where you to, boy, where you at?" – just as if I was back at home in Clevedon! The skipper said at one engagement, "I was listening to the marine radio last night to fishermen chatting to each other. It could have been, by the accent, anywhere in Cornwall, and as usual, being fishermen, I didn't understand a word they were saying!"

It was this link to the 'old country' that again was so important. People could look at the *Matthew* and see where they had come from. They could see how this island had developed from those early fishermen from Bristol, from Ireland, from the Basque regions and from France – and how they had become descendants of the European peoples in a new continent. Like all great journeys, we soon began sadly to realise that we had only two or three ports left to call. As we left Red Bay in Labrador, in torrential rain, with thick fog travelling at 30 knots as well as the rain, and into some heavy seas we thought, 'yes, we know it's not supposed to be like this with wind, fog and rain at the same time', but there it was. Suddenly, the sun broke through and the wind went down to about 26 knots. David Alan-Williams – a racing skipper by nature – felt the omens were good and we put all available sail up and broke the world record for medieval caravels, hitting a magic 9.3 knots!

With sails fully up and on a very close reach we finally headed into Trinity – our last port of call. It was estimated that 30,000 people were there to greet us and the same number when we left the next day. With our cannons firing from the ship, with fireworks from the shore, we slipped out of Trinity for a quiet few unannounced days in the capital, St John's, to make the ship clean and ready for the winter and the journey to Nova Scotia and Toronto."

86

NOVA SCOTIA AND EASTERN SEABOARD

With new supplies and some new crew on board, including Rodney and Mary North who had flown in from Bristol, the *Matthew* slipped out of St John's at 0500 on August 13, 1997. For her passage south, she was accompanied by the Canadian Coast Guard vessel the *Earl Grey* until she reached US waters two weeks later.

After three days at sea, the Nova Scotia coastline was spotted – St Paul's Island could be picked out some 25 miles away. As the *Matthew* was ahead of its arrival schedule, David Alan-Williams instructed the crew to give the ship a major summer overhaul. Saloon timbers were removed, scrubbed, hosed-down and dried; the bilges and the galley were cleaned and the deck timbers were hand-scrubbed with abrasive pads and wire wool before being finished off with a dose of Oxalic Acid to bleach them. By the time Neil's Harbour was reached the following morning, the *Matthew* was again looking picture-perfect and she was greeted by a bag-pipe playing band and civic dignitaries. Some crew departed for Newfoundland and others came on board and immediately had a treat for lunch – snow crabs courtesy of local man David Donovan.

Next stop was Sydney and the conditions allowed the *Matthew* to arrive with a full set of sails much to the delight of the crowds lining the quay. Hundreds more people clambered on board and the crew attended a function at the nearby Sydney Sailing Club. The early morning departure for Baddeck was witnessed by a select group of native Nova Scotians including Kevin Chaisson, a well-known local musician. Passing Cranberry Point on her outward journey the *Matthew* entered the spectacular Bras d'Or Lakes and travelled through them all day including a lunch break at Baddeck before dropping anchor in a small creek at St Georges Cove – quite a sight and a great surprise for local campers, moored yachts and car passengers.

'Up Anchor' at dawn, the following day the *Matthew* completed her passage through the Lakes and after negotiating the lock at St Peters, pulled alongside to moor for a few hours. Two schoolgirls were intrigued at the history the *Matthew* represented and 10 year-old Tangy couldn't stop talking about the ship and touching her. Turns out she'd recently completed a school project on Cabot and the *Matthew* and was happy to be sent on her way with a souvenir piece of line from the rope locker! The still air and photogenic vistas were left behind as the crew set out for Halifax and the open sea once more.

Fog, mist and heavy rain greeted the *Matthew*'s arrival in Halifax at 1800 on 23 August. Donned in their medieval

Everyone had to muck in with scrubbing the deck!

THE MATTHEW

The Shelburne Re-enactment Association, including Sheila Firth, greet the Matthew

clothes that got very wet, the crew soon changed into drier gear ahead of another round of speeches and receptions. In the evening the Premier of Nova Scotia, Russell MacLellan, gave a cocktail party, the Lieutenant Governor gave another one at his colonial style residence and just for good measure the Royal Yacht Squadron followed up with a third! The following day there was a church service held at the main Anglican Church at which David Alan-Williams and St John Hartnell (who had flown in with his wife Sara) read the lessons. The Service was conducted by a Bristolian who had been a Methodist Minister in Fishponds in the 1960s. The service was followed by a Reception at the Maritime Museum and another local was found nearby by some of the crew when walking around outside - the *Marguerite T*, a beautifully restored Bristol Channel Pilot Cutter, built at Pill in 1893 and now some 3,000 miles from home!

From Halifax the next port of call was Shelburne and what a reception was in wait. Founded in 1783 by loyalists of the American Revolution, it retains much of its historical charm through preserved buildings and displays of living history. Waiting to greet the *Matthew* were members of the Shelburne Re-enactment Association, dressed in the uniform of the 3rd Battalion of the New Jersey Volunteers - a British regiment that fought during the Revolutionary War. There was much excitement in town as the *Matthew* arrived with an exchange of musketry and cannon fire. Among those greeting the ship and dressed in period puritan clothes was Sheila Firth, the local deaconess and John Firth, a drummer in the re-enactment group. The Norths were billeted with the Firths overnight, but before bedtime, there was a 'planked' public dinner of freshly smoked and unsmoked cooked salmon. For $10, locals could partake in the supper and take the opportunity of talking to the *Matthew* crew.

With some new crew on board and a good night's sleep behind them it was time to move on again. Yarmouth was reached on August 28 and it was time to say goodbye to the *Earl Grey*. The crew of the Canadian Coast Guard escort vessel hosted a farewell reception and inspection on board their ship for the *Matthew* crew. There was a large and enthusiastic gathering to see off the *Matthew* from Yarmouth the following day, including the Firths who were spotted in the crowd.

The *Matthew* now left Canadian waters for a while and sailed to Bath in Maine in the United States and came alongside the jetty near the Maine Maritime Museum. It was here on August 31, 1997, that the occupants of a passing motor boat informed the crew of the *Matthew* that Diana, Princess of Wales had been killed in a car crash in Paris. As a mark of respect, the Red Ensign was flown half-masted from then until her funeral.

After three days in Bath, the *Matthew* made her way to Manchester-by-the-Sea in Massachusetts where dozens of men, women and children from the Cabot family clan came on board. This branch of the Cabots can reputedly trace their origins to another John Cabot who emigrated from Jersey in 1700 and are regarded as one of Boston's oldest families. An evening reception and dinner was laid on by John Cabot, head of the Cabot Corporation and the following morning several members of the extended family joined as crew for the short passage to Boston as Mrs Cabot clambered up to the crow's nest!

Now dressed in their medieval clothes, the crew arrived to a thunderous welcome and fired off a few cannon rounds that rattled nearby skyscraper windows. The *Matthew* had pride of place alongside the New England Aquarium. Joining in the fun was Courtenay Cabot who joined as a crew member and helped on the passage up the St Lawrence.

After getting as far south as Bristol, Rhode Island, Matthew was booked to be the centrepiece of a major exhibition of Canadian culture, under cover on the Toronto Harbourfront. However, having struggled up the St Lawrence, and taken in Quebec City and Montreal, the *Matthew* encountered some of the most testing and uncomfortable seas of the whole year on Lake Ontario, and the show never materialised. Whilst in Canada, the *Matthew* had to earn its keep and cover its costs. It did this through being chartered by the various Canadian provinces and towns to visit as well as public donations on board.

For its over-wintering, Port Credit Yacht Club on Lake Ontario offered an ideal on-the-water haven for the *Matthew*

A wintery scene greeted the *Matthew* in Toronto

and as a bonus, the water was ice-free owing in part to a very mild winter and to the warmth generated by an adjacent power station. After de-rigging all but the masts and storing supplies and equipment in a 40 foot container, the ship was 'winterised' – leaving Terry Nash in charge as caretaker over the winter months. During this time he hosted many corporate dinners on board that were another useful source of income. Meanwhile James Roy and David Alan-Williams took a break away in England as engineer Russell Thiessen said farewell and departed for Tasmania.

The *Matthew* berthed at Quai Jacques Cartier in the centre of Montreal

RETURN LEG AND HOMEWARD BOUND

In April 1998, the skipper and James Roy returned to move the *Matthew* the seven miles from the Yacht Club to the Toronto Harbourfront to open the ship for public boarding, and to enable the crew to continue with the maintenance programme.

At this point original crew member Mark Chislett re-joined as ship's carpenter and following 'an offer he couldn't understand' was promoted to Second Mate and Watch Captain as well as Chief Gunner for the return voyage. One of his first jobs was to refit the cabin windows in order to meet Canadian sea worthiness and insurance standards. At the same time, Mark Drew joined as ship's engineer. Originally from Melksham, he was visiting friends having previously worked on a schooner at the local dry dock in Toronto. During a chance conversation over a beer or two with James Roy, he was signed-up.

Wednesday May 20, 1998, was the official send off from Toronto and the start of the journey back home to Bristol. The ship returned briefly to Port Credit Yacht Club so that the supplies and equipment stored in the large container could be retrieved and returned to the ship. From here, the *Matthew* set out for Hamilton where several thousand visitors boarded the ship and then on to Port Dalhousie for a five-day stop-over where another 4,000 visitors clambered on board. Heading north back across Lake Ontario, the landmarks of Toronto were highlighted by the setting sun and the recorded log passed the 12,000 mile mark since the March 1996 sea trials. At Oshawa during a two-day stop-over, another 6,000 or so people came on board – numbers that matched the previous year's daily totals. The extraordinary interest in the ship continued.

From Oshawa, Kingston was reached after a 115 mile overnight passage and close to Fort Henry there was an exchange of cannon fire as a salute. The *Matthew* berthed at the Kingston Maritime Museum on the Lakes and in the

The *Matthew*'s crow's nest shows a striking resemblance to Toronto's CN Tower

THE MATTHEW

The vast expanse of the St Lawrence River

evening the crew was hosted by the local Mayor. Around 3,500 visitors boarded the ship and there was a spectacular display by the Canadian Air Force's 'Snow Birds' aerobatic team overhead.

The departure from Kingston marked the passing from Lake Ontario into the St Lawrence River Seaway and early next morning John Jack Smith re-joined the ship off Brockville in order to sail on to Prescott. Passing through the lock system of the St Lawrence Seaway was eventful with some locks featuring drops of 70 feet. Once through Snell Lock the *Matthew* followed channel markers but the watch on deck didn't appreciate the force and direction of flow. Before they could respond *Matthew* was swept out of the marked channel and at 0140 ran aground. Despite valiant attempts by the crew to free her, she would not budge. Roger Lalonde from the Coast Guard auxiliary heard the ship's predicament over the radio and came alongside in a small launch and eventually a line was taken from the masthead and the ship was towed off its temporary berth. The damage to the keel would be revealed later, but there were no leaks. Nearly nine hours later the *Matthew* was on her way again and after negotiating three further locks arrived in Montreal another 12 hours on. The crew was exhausted, but not too tired to fire some cannons that reverberated along the sides of Quai Jacques Cartier in the middle of the harbour. The *Matthew* was well visited in Montreal and there was an exchange of presentations with Mayor Pierre Bourque.

Next up was Quebec City which, with no more locks, was reached after an enjoyable downstream passage in sunshine. Here the crew prepared for the first long passage of the season and a return to salt water. Meanwhile, as the *Matthew* was preparing to leave Quebec City, another Matthew was being christened in Bonavista Harbour. Under Newfoundland's Matthew Legacy Committee and built by master shipbuilder Wayne Marsh and his team, to the designs of naval architect Leonard Pecore, Newfoundland and Labrador's own wooden Matthew was designed to be a floating museum piece and to form part of a permanent interpretation centre in Bonavista. Local volunteer Frances Sweetland was on hand to christen the vessel and Newfoundlander Chris LeGrow, a crew member who made the North Atlantic crossing the year before, was made 'Honorary Captain' for the day.

Leaving Quebec City and heading east along the St Lawrence, the banks got further apart until they could not be seen one from the other. Passing the Gaspe headland a new course south was set for New Brunswick and before arriving at Miramichi the crew was reminded that they were no longer sailing on a flat lake as the wind kicked up a bad-tempered sea, with fog and rain. Overnight from Miramichi, the *Matthew* arrived at Charlottetown, on Canada Day and 125 years after Prince Edward Island had joined the Canadian Confederation.

Next was Port Hawkesbury for an overnight stop and participation in a music festival. Dressed in their medieval clothes, the crew joined the carnival procession and posed on a Lions Club playground pirate ship. By July 10, 1998, the *Matthew* was alongside Royal Cape Breton Yacht Club, Sydney, where it welcomed back Paul Venton who had flown in from Bristol to be part of the return crew – one of six who completed both North Atlantic crossings.

The *Matthew* continued to re-trace its steps from the previous August. It had already renewed its acquaintance with Baddeck and a 'magic evening sail out of Bras D'Or Lake' was further enhanced by a deck feast of 36 freshly cooked lobsters!

The *Matthew* left Nova Scotia behind and headed for St John's Harbour in Newfoundland in readiness for its return across the North Atlantic. It was a good opportunity to test

THANK YOU FROM CANADA

To show the nation's appreciation, Danielle Wetherup, Master of the Royal Canadian Mint, wrote to crew members… "I would like to take this opportunity to thank you for your work with the *Matthew* during 1997. It was a remarkable achievement to recreate and sail a ship with the techniques of a bygone era. Your contribution to the success of the *Matthew* project is sincerely appreciated by the thousands of Canadians who flocked to Canadian ports to see the *Matthew*. Canadians truly marvelled at the beauty of the ship and the skills of the crews who sailed her. As a token of appreciation on behalf of all Canadians, please accept this plaque mounted with a sterling silver ten cent coin depicting *Matthew*. The sterling silver coin was minted by the Royal Canadian Mint to commemorate the 500th anniversary of Giovanni Caboto's to North America."

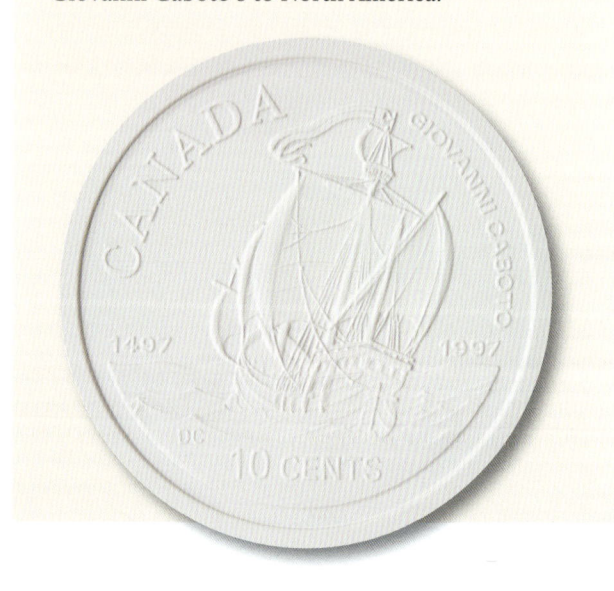

Commemorative phone cards were popular souvenirs for the crew

the bilge pumps, to clean the hold, to test the water maker and the myriad of other maintenance tasks and 'man over board' routines ahead of the crossing. With all sails set including the topsail, a good fair wind and the sun shining brightly, the ship was under sail power alone and the day's sail was regarded as the best of the year up to then. To add to the delight of the crew they witnessed a spectacular show from humpback whales and Atlantic white sided dolphins engaged in a feeding frenzy.

When the wind faded after sunset, the *Matthew* slow-motored into St John's just after sunrise. Just to make sure everyone knew *Matthew* was in town a few well-aimed rounds were fired from the cannon. Anyone still asleep would be awakened by the din. James Roy, freshly returned from his sister's wedding, was waiting on the quayside to take the lines.

The Dockyard at St John's wasted little time in lifting the ship out of the water in order to inspect and antifoul

HOMEWARD BOUND

The cost of the return trip was sponsored by Crest Homes to the tune of £100,000. Crest was in the middle of re-developing part of Bristol's Harbourside and this was a highly visible promotional opportunity for the company. At the time, the future of the *Matthew* was uncertain. Some believed the return transatlantic voyage would be the last time she would sail the oceans as it was mooted that she would become a static museum piece in Bristol. For now though, all the crew was interested in was sailing the ship home as quickly as possible and perhaps beating Cabot's return journey time of 15 days.

The return crew comprised 12 British, five Canadians and two Americans - including six who had made the first Atlantic crossing and 13 other men and women. Several had been among the 500 or so people who had sailed the *Matthew* whilst it was in North America. These included Gordon Sloane from Ontario who had become 'enchanted with the ship' when he crewed her the previous winter; and Courtenay Cabot from Boston who had sailed up the St Lawrence on the ship the previous year – and who had organised for the *Matthew* to be a flag carrier for the United Nations Year of the Oceans. On her crew data sheet, she explained her reasons for wishing to be one of the crew for the return to Bristol... "This voyage means a lot to me – primarily because I love this ship and the crew that is sailing her." Very prophetic words. Right next to her crew data sheet was that of Bristol's Paul Venton. They dated on the return trip and were married in Massachusetts in 2003 where they live in Courtenay's family home along with their three children. What a lovely story and no wonder the *Matthew* holds a special place in their hearts…

Meanwhile, back to the departure. One year, one month and one day after arriving in Newfoundland, the final shore line was cast off by Tourism Minister Sandra Kelly and

Some of the crew enjoy a relaxing lunch on deck

underneath and repair the keel damaged when the *Matthew* ran aground. Some replacement timbers using North American oak were required and the shipwrights finished the job within 48 hours – leaving the crew to sand and varnish the hull and deck rails prior to a second coat of antifouling and launching two days later.

Now looking a picture, whilst alongside at the Dockyard, many *Matthew* friends and the Newfoundland Cabot 500 team from the year before came on board. Laurel Alan-Williams and David Redfern had flown in to be present for the departure and as most of the crew were taking a day or so to sort themselves out for the voyage, the food provisioning team was getting frantic. With a rolling seven-day menu to source Laurel Alan-Williams and crew member Stephanie Booth from Clevedon were busily stacking food into daily piles in the front room of the local Bonne Esperance B&B, that quickly resembled a corner shop rather than a guest house.

THE MATTHEW

Son of Town Hall on its way to Ireland

the *Matthew* slowly made her way towards the harbour entrance. Accompanied by a cacophony of sound from car and ship horns, fireworks, blasts from the ship's cannons and cheers from thousands of people, the *Matthew* bid farewell to Newfoundland. The sails were set, the motor was turned off, and as Fort Amhurst was passed, the clock started at 0145 UTC (Co-ordinated Universal Time) on July 26 to see if the *Matthew* could equal the time of 15 days that John Cabot achieved for his return journey some 501 years earlier.

The return journey was not without incident. If anyone thought that sailing the *Matthew* across the Atlantic was foolhardy, then a distress alert from the Halifax Rescue Centre put things into perspective. The alert was for *Son of Town Hall* – a 40 foot house boat raft with four adults and three dogs on board. Crewed by the 'Floating Neutrinos' – Poppa Neutrino (David Pearlman) and his wife Capt Betsy (Betsy Terrell) and their friends Ed Garry and Roger Doncaster, the houseboat had been assembled along the waterfront in New York. Using logs and drift wood plucked from the Hudson River and recycled materials from the streets and garbage bins of Manhattan, it was apparently seaworthy. *Son of Town Hall* had left Newfoundland on June 15.

Its two most important features were the ability to self-right if tipped over, and to self-steer in storms. The self-steering feature was supposed to keep the raft always pointed in a direction that avoided the possibility of being tipped over by waves. Well that was the theory. The *Matthew* received several updates on the progress of the raft, the final one being from the Falmouth Coastguard when a Pan Pan call was received to warn of a potential problem on board, but no immediate danger. Sixty days after leaving Newfoundland, *Son of Town Hall* arrived safely and to a hero's welcome at Castletown Bearhaven in Ireland, from where the *Matthew* had departed the year before.

Back to the *Matthew*, and light winds early in the voyage scuppered any chance of beating Cabot's return journey time of 15 days. However, in one day of milestones - August 8 - the *Matthew* averaged more than six knots over a 24-hour period for the first time; she achieved 147 miles under sail alone and she went beyond 15,000 miles travelled since her launch.

As the *Matthew* neared the French coast, the skipper was in reflective mood, "It is a tribute to the boat builders that constructed her on the dockside in Bristol that she is still as sound now as she was then. The hull lines drawn by Colin Mudie have proven to be well balanced and his keen artistic eye has created a vessel of beauty that attracts everyone's attention. *Matthew* is a good ship that has sailed a lot of miles and has the potential for many more."

A few days later on August 13, and 18 days after leaving St John's, the *Matthew* made its way through the narrow entrance to Port Rhu Harbour, in time for the Dournanez Maritime Festival in Brittany where she joined 1,000 other boats. Safely berthed to the applause of hundreds of people on the quayside, it was time for some farewells as several crew left the ship to return to their homes and their day jobs. Other volunteer crew arrived to take their places

RETURN LEG AND HOMEWARD BOUND

A triumphant return to Bristol – past the *SS Great Britain* and then through the Merchants Road swingbridge

and after the Dournanez Festival, the *Matthew* headed for Weymouth and Lymington and then on to Portsmouth where she starred in the Second International Festival of the Sea.

From Portsmouth, the *Matthew* made stops at Falmouth, Cardiff and Clevedon before she made a triumphant and emotional return to Bristol Harbour on September 12, 1998. After three years as skipper it was time for David Alan-Williams to depart. He had done a great job and had another project in the offing – this time to project manage the construction of the Italian America's Cup yachts. As he left, the keys to the *Matthew* were handed to Mark Chislett who was made Shore Captain of the *Matthew* for the next 12 months pending a decision on the ship's future. The ship was berthed alongside the *SS Great Britain* and the Lord Mayor hosted a meeting of interested parties to discuss future plans for the *Matthew*. Once the administrative and financial arrangements had been resolved, the SS Great Britain Trust agreed to take the *Matthew* under its wing and her immediate future was secured.

Mark Chislett becomes 'shore captain' on the *Matthew*'s return

97

A storm looms as the *Matthew* is tethered to a buoy off Clovelly

21ST CENTURY MATTHEW

When the *Matthew* returned to Bristol in 1998 there was a thought that she may end up as a permanent and static museum piece. Thankfully, that has not been the case and she continues to function as an operational sailing ship – delighting and thrilling everyone who sails her and creating a wonderful spectacle wherever she ventures. She's a real ambassador for Bristol.

The annual maintenance programme has ensured she's kept in great shape and this has allowed her to clock up thousands of nautical miles since her return from Newfoundland. She's explored the seas around Britain and Ireland – taking paying passengers as well as volunteers and youth groups – and has attended dozens of maritime festivals around the UK and France where she's been a popular attraction in Normandy, Brittany and further down the French west coast.

SELECTION OF ADVENTURES SINCE 1998

2001 – First trip for paying passengers. A two-month passage taking in Portishead, Penzance, Plymouth, Weymouth, St Vaast la Hougue in Normandy, Cowes, Portsmouth for the Festival of the Sea, Dartmouth, Penzance, St Ives, Lundy and Swansea. Skippered by Nigel Ottley, the crew included Luke Porter and James Roy who sailed the North Atlantic with *Matthew* in 1997.

2003 – An 11-week passage to Scotland, Ireland and Wales; including stops at Oban, Loch na Keal, Talbet, Campbell Town, Liverpool (where *Matthew* featured at the Mersey River Festival), Dun Laoghaire, Youghal, Crosshaven, Milford Haven, Skomer and Swansea. On board passengers included a school party from Bristol accompanied by their teachers. Several of the children had learning difficulties and the trip was a positive experience for all of them – although one child needed urgent hospitalisation with appendicitis!

2004 – A 30-day passage to France, taking in a wine festival in Bordeaux and the Festival of the Sea in Brest. The trip marked the 100th anniversary of the Entente Cordiale – the treaty signed between France and England. An oak sapling grown from an acorn from Leigh Woods, near Bristol, was presented on arrival in Bordeaux, a city twinned with Bristol. The *Matthew* was made an honorary member of the

Skipper Nigel Ottley with oak saplings bound for Bordeaux

THE MATTHEW

Grand Conseil du Vin de Bordeaux and there was the usual exchange of plaques and gifts.

2006 – An end of May departure from Bristol saw the *Matthew* take in Irish destinations including Dublin, Arklow, Dun Laoghaire, Clogherhead, Warrenpoint, Carlingford, Bangor and Carrickfergus. Then on to Ramsey, Isle of Man and Whitehaven in Cumbria before sailing around the Western Iles of Scotland including Loch Fyne and Mull of Kintyre. Next up was Glasgow before the return journey to Bristol – eventually arriving home at the end of July. Skippered by Rob Salvidge, the crew for part of the passage, included volunteers Roger Gough and Shawn Spencer-Smith.

2007 – Two passages along the Somerset and Devon coasts to Ilfracombe; a trip along the Welsh coast for Bristol Scouts; a trip to the Tall Ships Festival in Gloucester Docks via the Sharpness Canal and a passage along the English Channel to London - for over-wintering at St Katherine's Dock near Tower Bridge and an opportunity to raise the awareness of the ship on the 10th anniversary of her first North Atlantic crossing.

2011 – For two weeks in April, the *Matthew* put in an appearance at the National Maritime Museum in Falmouth and the following month was in Penzance where a crew of pirates held the Lord Mayor hostage on the ship as part of the town's attempt to break the world record for the number of pirates on a promenade! A world record was indeed set and thousands of pounds was raised for the RNLI.

2012 – In the spring, the *Matthew* spent two months visiting ports in Cornwall and in May, she sailed to St Mary's on the Scilly Isles to bring Bristol-based rowers to the World Pilot Gig Championships. She also acted as a floating hotel for some of the competitors. In June, the *Matthew*, along with

The *Matthew* flying Jolly Roger flags opposite the Tower of London in 2007

its companion, the *Pyronaut* represented Bristol among the vessels taking part in the Queen's Diamond Jubilee Pageant in London. The *Matthew* was moored on the Thames in an *Avenue of Sail* for vessels too large to go under the bridges along the Thames.

2013 – The Vannes Maritime Festival in Brittany in May was skipper Rick Wakeham's first long passage in the *Matthew*. All was well on the voyage from Bristol to the French port, but the return experience was more akin to the frightening North Atlantic storm experienced by the 1997 crew. The original intention was to return via Newlyn, but in mid-channel, the *Matthew* hit violent, storm force 11 conditions with big 30 feet seas and gusts of up to 85 knots. For five hours the beam of the ship was angled into the waves, and with a loose line fouling both props, speed was limited to around two knots. The ship drifted eastwards and much to the relief of all on board the storm subsided and the *Matthew* made it safely into Falmouth. Quite a baptism for the new skipper and his crew!

2016 – The longest seagoing trip of the year was to Padstow in Cornwall where the ship received thousands of visitors. Even when closed to visitors there were crowds of people sometimes five-deep keen to ask questions about the ship. The crew was comprised mostly of volunteers who, despite plenty of sea sickness on board had a swell time! The shortest seagoing passage was across the Bristol Channel where the *Matthew* starred as the Ancient Mariner's ship for the Coleridge in Wales Festival 2016 - sailing into Cardiff Bay and then on to Swansea's Prince of Wales Dock. Here there were tours of the ship, which was themed around Coleridge's poem *The Rime of the Ancient Mariner*. The *Matthew* was complete with a ghost crew of zombies, scorched decks and the Ancient Mariner himself carrying a dead albatross!

Tall ships photographed from the *Matthew* during the Dublin Maritime Festival

The *Matthew* on the slip at Underfall Yard in 2017

Matthew volunteers, members of The Matthew of Bristol Trust and skipper Rick Wakeham (red sweater) in 2017

THE MATTHEW VOLUNTEERS

As with many charitable trusts it is often the work of volunteers, much of which goes unseen, that keeps things going. Operating and maintaining a wooden ship has its challenges and it is the dedication and passion of more than 30 Matthew volunteers that keeps the ship afloat and keeps it looking 'Ship Shape and Bristol Fashion'.

In January each year the *Matthew* undergoes her annual maintenance programme at the magnificent Underfall Yard in Bristol where she is hauled out of the water, for a few days or maybe a week. If timbers need replacing this is the time it is done and volunteers can be seen anti-fouling the undersides, removing barnacles, cleaning, scrubbing, sanding, oiling and painting the ship. Other volunteers check pumps, the electrics, the heads, the navigation equipment and the engine to make sure all's well for the upcoming programme of harbour cruises and ocean passages. It's like an annual MOT but a little more complicated than that. To keep costs down, most jobs are done in-house and the work is followed by an annual inspection by the Maritime and Coastguard Agency. This comprises an in water and out of water survey with risk assessments updated and records thoroughly checked. Getting through this inspection allows the granting of a licence to carry passengers and the certification of sea worthiness for a further year.

Aside from repairs and maintenance tasks, volunteers keep their skills up by attending First Aid and Firefighting courses; they act as guides for visits by school parties and members of the public; they help to crew the ship during harbour cruises and on longer passages at sea, and they help when the ship is on hire to individuals and to companies. They also help with renovating the concrete barge the *Matthew* is moored against and Matthew volunteers also produce Visitor Guides, give presentations to local schools and societies and have starred as extras when the *Matthew* is used by production companies for documentaries and television and movie productions.

The volunteers are passionate about their *Matthew*:

"The *Matthew* is a Bristol 'icon' and I love the feel of the *Matthew*, and all the history that goes with her."

"She is the only operational caravel in the world and really does sail. Along with the volunteers, she makes a considerable contribution to the profile of the Port of Bristol."

"I love meeting the wide variety of visitors from the four corners of the earth."

"I enjoy learning the art of medieval sailing and putting this knowledge to use to help others learn about sailing in Tudor times."

"What is so special about the *Matthew*? Well, in order of preference - when she goes to sea, when she goes out, when she stays in, when I am near her, when I talk about her, when I read about her, and when I read her history, I could go on but won't!"

Schoolchildren learning the art of medieval navigation

EDUCATION

School parties are very welcome visitors to the *Matthew* and dozens of groups come on board between March and November each year. Principally aimed at primary school children, there are three types of one-hour trips. Designed to fit in with Key Stages 1 and 2 of the National Curriculum,

THE MATTHEW

Matthew pictured alongside Riverstation Bar & Kitchen during the wedding breakfast for Eloise King and Christopher Wilson, October 6, 2012

subjects covered include local history, John Cabot and the discovery of Newfoundland, and what it would have been like on board a Tudor sailing ship. Citizenship, leisure and tourism, and drama studies can also be accommodated and school parties are also able to study the life of the notorious Bristol-born pirate Edward Teach or Thatch – better known as Blackbeard. Blackbeard and his crew of pirates terrorised sailors and raided ships in the Atlantic Ocean and Caribbean Sea in the early part of the 18th century.

Leading the groups, the *Matthew* volunteers take great delight in engaging children with the history of the *Matthew* and life as a medieval sailor. The educational sessions are run on board the *Matthew* and as well as allowing pupils to explore the ship, they get to experience it in action as it cruises around Bristol harbour while the session takes place. The three one-hour sessions are:

Pirates Designed for reception, year 1 and year 2 children. Children come on board for a 45-minute adventure around the historic Bristol harbour on a real life pirate ship. They learn about Blackbeard and his scary pirate friends and even hoist the Jolly Roger flag!

1st Mate Aimed at Years 3 – 6, pupils become part of the *Matthew*'s crew for a 45 minute trip around the harbour and learn about life on board in Tudor times; how sailors sailed the ship then, and how it is done today.

Deckhand Ideal for larger groups, sessions takes place on board the *Matthew* while she remains moored at the quayside. Pupils step aboard and learn about Tudor life at sea. How did sailors navigate across unknown and treacherous seas to undiscovered lands? Why did they go? What were they trying to find and exactly where did they end up? The Captain and volunteer crew literally show pupils the ropes and how to tie them and show them how things work down below deck as well.

Although accommodating less able-bodied pupils and adults presents some challenges on board, the *Matthew*'s mooring outside M Shed does allow for wheelchair access to the main deck. The volunteers have welcomed many children with special educational needs on board and have had very positive feedback from the children and their carers, including this testimonial from the Special Friends Club in Bristol, "I am sure you can imagine for many families taking a child with special needs is a daunting prospect. Your staff were amazing, totally understanding and so calm. Every member of staff went the extra mile to make this a truly memorable experience. A huge thank you from us to all and every one of you. As I said an amazing day and one of the best days out we have been on. Thank you, thank you, thank you..."

HARBOUR CRUISES, CHARTERS AND EVENT HIRE

The *Matthew* has to pay her way and much of her income comes from local cruises and corporate and private hire events. A unique venue for corporate events, the ship can host catered harbour trips, quayside champagne and canapes receptions and corporate family fun trips.

Captain Barnacle and his Pirate Pantomime

Companies also use the ship for teambuilding events where participants form part of the ship's crew for a three-hour session that takes in various on-board challenges with an emphasis on team work as well as a trip round the harbour. Whether it be a wedding reception or a sea-shanty accompanied silver wedding anniversary, the *Matthew* is a popular venue for families to hold celebratory events.

A timetable of harbour cruise events is scheduled from March to November each year. These include Fish & Chip supper cruises, sometimes accompanied by one of the resident Sea Shanty groups; trips around the harbour or down the Avon Gorge; summer Cream Tea trips and special Mother's Day and Father's Day cruises. During the spring and summer months, Captain Barnacle can also be seen on board. Popular with adults as well as children, the Pirate Pantomime provides a rip roaring on board trip with the show featuring plenty of pirate props, puppet hilarity, comedy, and lashings of audience participation, silliness and banter.

THE MATTHEW

The *Dawn Treader* making her way along the Avon Gorge (top) and arriving in Falmouth (bottom)

FILM AND TELEVISION

Ever since the start of construction work on Redcliffe Wharf in 1994, the *Matthew* has featured in dozens of film and television productions. For the well-loved ship this is a significant area of work and a welcome source of income. Channel 4's 'Time Team' and light entertainment offerings such as the BBC's 'The Hairy Bikers', 'Don't Tell the Bride' and 'Celebrity Antiques Road Trip' have all filmed sequences on the ship. Hardly a year goes by without some film, drama or documentary work coming the *Matthew*'s way.

Projects have included:

2007 Promotional work for Disney and the launch of the 'Pirates of the Caribbean' DVD whilst the ship was in London. A treasure chest full of pretend money was placed on deck and one lucky Capital Radio listener won that amount in real money – around £40,000!

2008 The movie 'Broadside'. A day's filming took place on the ship in the September of that year – on the same day as the Bristol Half Marathon. This caused the sound engineer a few headaches with the background noise!

2009 Historian Dan Snow followed in his father's footsteps (Peter Snow) by filming on the *Matthew* in Bristol Harbour and at sea during the making of the BBC2 documentary series 'Empire of the Seas'. Talking about his experience on the *Matthew* he said, "As I hoisted the sails, I was overwhelmed by what a daunting experience it must have been to venture into the unknown. Yet it was that spirit of discovery and endeavour that led to Britain becoming the greatest naval power the world had ever seen."

2010 During the year the *Matthew* featured in an episode of the BBC4 documentary series 'The Boats that Built Britain.' In complete contrast, she was also transformed to act as a double and was chartered for promotional work for 'Chronicles of Narnia: The Voyage of the Dawn Treader'. Her journey from Bristol to Cornwall turned heads wherever she went. Over the August Bank Holiday, the National Maritime Museum in Falmouth played host to a Chronicles of Narnia weekend where visitors could come on board.

21ST CENTURY MATTHEW

Bristol band, A Doubtful Sound, on board for a music video

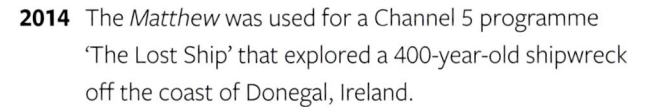

Celebrating the 20th anniversary of the *Matthew*'s voyage to Newfoundland

2014 The *Matthew* was used for a Channel 5 programme 'The Lost Ship' that explored a 400-year-old shipwreck off the coast of Donegal, Ireland.

2015 An ABC Disney production of 'Galavant' boarded the ship in the December and featured a guest appearance by Hugh Bonneville who played Peter the Pillager, the Pirate King. In the same year, Bristol band, 'A Doubtful Sound', filmed a promotional music video for their new EP, 'Kids'.

2016 The *Matthew* was hired for location work during filming of the Bill Kenwright Films production of 'Another Mother's Son' when Princes Wharf outside M Shed was turned into a massive film set.

A FINAL WORD

As guests and volunteers came together to celebrate the 20th anniversary of the re-enactment of the modern *Matthew*'s voyage to Newfoundland in 1997, it is striking that although young in historical terms, the much loved little ship has developed a fascinating history all of her own. There's tremendous affection for the *Matthew*,

The *Matthew* passing beneath the Clifton Suspension Bridge on an Avon Gorge trip

not only in Bristol where she's a real ambassador for the city, but in North America, particularly Canada where she also has iconic status. From the germ of an idea in a city council committee meeting in the 1980s, to one of Bristol's greatest present-day treasures, it has been a joy to recount just a fraction of the many tales of the *Matthew* of Bristol. She will surely add even more colourful chapters to her story in the years ahead.

To coin Newfoundland seafaring slang...
"Long may her big jib draw."

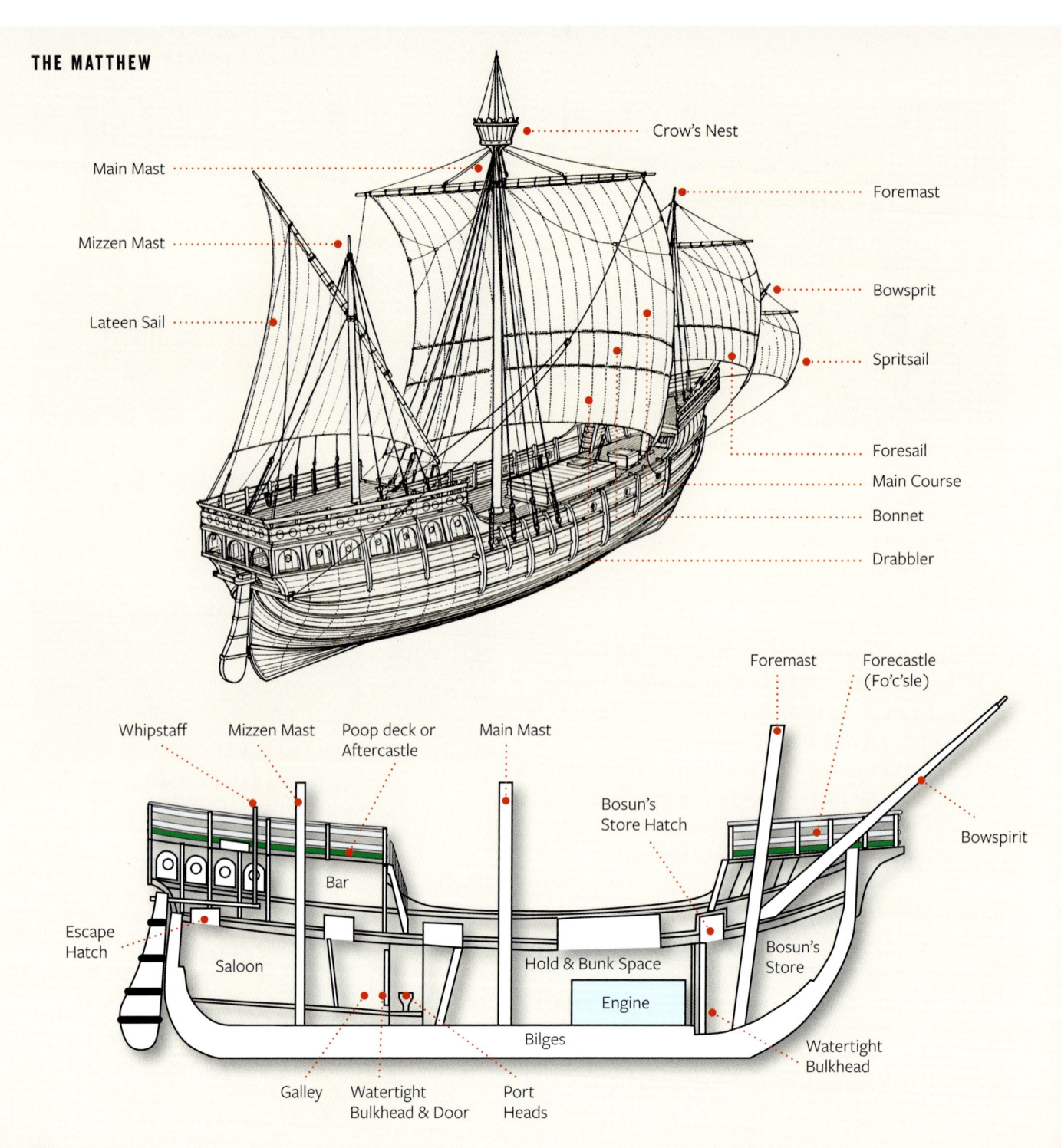

THE MATTHEW

108

ABOUT THE MATTHEW OF BRISTOL

MAIN DECK

The main deck stretches from the bow (front) to the stern (rear). Towards the bow, there is a raised deck – the Fo'c'sle (or forecastle) and towards the stern there is another raised deck – called the Aftercastle. These raised decks were, in medieval times, literally castles, which were added to ships to enable soldiers to fight as though they were ashore in real castles. Access to the two castles is via ladders.

The 15th century *Matthew* was a cargo vessel capable of transporting up to 50 large barrels (tuns), each of which could hold around one cubic metre of wine, olive oil, soap and other commodities. These tuns were put down below in the hold – the very large hatch on the main deck provided access to the hold.

Right in the middle of the main deck is the main mast which carries the main sail (or main course). The main sail is laced to the main yard which is normally horizontal when the ship is sailing – the yard plus the sail weighs approximately 500kgs and it takes up to eight crewmen to raise and set the sail. Above the main course is the main topsail.

Forward of the main deck on the fo'c'sle is the foremast with its rectangular foresail and aft is the mizzen mast with the triangular lateen sail. Right in the front of the ship is the bowsprit. It has a small rectangular sail called the spritsail.

It is important to note that crewmen do not have to go aloft to set the sails – everything can be accomplished from deck level. There are literally kilometres of rope on the ship and crewmen need to know what every single rope does – this is "learning the ropes"; there are halyards, braces, sheets, tack lines, bunt lines, martinets and so on. When the various ropes have been hauled in, they are tied off on pinrails or kevels.

At the after end of the main deck is an enclosed area where a cabin houses all the modern navigation instruments and charts. Behind the cabin is the tiller with its whip staff. Steering normally takes place on the deck above.

On the port side towards the bow and under the fo'c'sle, is the electrically-driven anchor windlass with the anchor itself on the main deck, below the port ladder to the fo'c'sle. There is also a stern anchor which is normally stowed on the rail at the after end of the after castle deck.

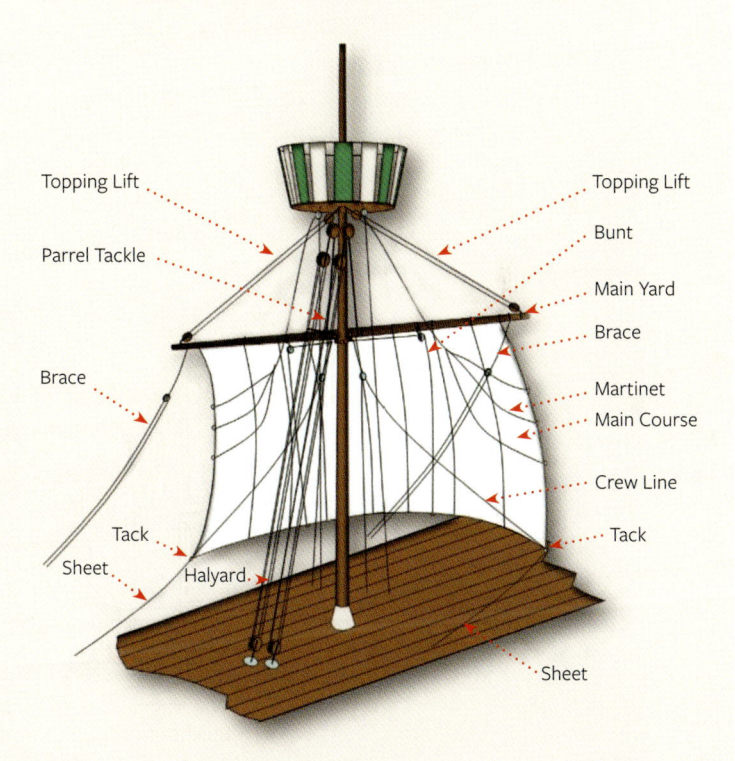

109

AFTER DECK

The raised after deck, the Aftercastle, has a number of important functions. Firstly, the skipper or watch keeper can get a good view of the ship and the surrounding waters. Secondly, during normal cruising conditions, the after deck is the location of the main steering position. The helmsman can steer the ship by means of the Whip Staff, a long pole which is situated just astern of the Mizzen Mast. The Whip Staff is connected, via a hole in the after deck, to the tiller (on the deck below) which in turn is connected to the rudder. To turn to port, the helmsman pushes the Whip Staff to the left or vice versa to the right, to turn to starboard.

This after deck, in later years, was called the Quarter Deck and very often there was a religious shrine mounted in a prominent position.

The rearmost mast on the ship, the Mizzen Mast, is located on the after deck and all associated ropes for the sail can be controlled from this deck. All ropes are tied off on Pin Rails. There are similar pin rails for the Main Mast, Foremast and the bowsprit. Unlike the other principal sails on the *Matthew*, the mizzen sail is referred to as a Lateen Sail.

THE FO'C'SLE

The fo'c'sle (or forecastle) is a short deck above the forward part of the main deck accessible using two ladders. It is on this deck that the crew has access to the bowsprit (along with its spritsail) and the foremast and foresail. The foremast is raked forward. The main reason for this is to allow the foot of the foremast to be stepped on the keel, not the curved stem.

Under the fo'c'sle (forecastle), on the main deck level, spare ropes and other ready-to-use items are stowed. The anchor windlass is also there.

FLAGS

There are normally two flags flown from the after deck. Firstly the Red Ensign, a red background flag with the Union Flag in the upper quarter next to the hoist. This is the flag flown by UK merchant vessels and private yachts. Secondly, the Tudor Ensign, which has a background of green and white stripes (Tudor colours) and the cross of St George in the upper quadrant next to the hoist.

BELOW DECKS

Beneath the main deck is the hold in which the medieval *Matthew* carried its cargo in very large barrels called "tuns". There was no room for the crew to sleep below decks so they had to curl up on the main deck wherever they could find a dry and sheltered space. Today in the hold are 18 bunks for the crew, an enclosed space for the engine and two lavatories (called "Heads"). Aft of this compartment is a modern galley equipped with refrigerators, a gas stove and other items to enable the crew to eat well. There is also a large table.

FIGUREHEAD

The ship's first figurehead, a Talbot dog, was lost at sea some years before the present one was fitted in 2015. Made by Bristol wood carver, Michael Henderson, the White Greyhound of Richmond is one of the Queen's Beasts and bears a shield of white and green Tudor livery, with a Tudor Rose ensigned by a Royal Crown. Henry VII sometimes used greyhounds as supporters and on his standards. His father, Edmund Tudor, was created Earl of Richmond and the white greyhound was associated with the Honour of Richmond. The rose in the badge shows the association of the red and the white elements of Lancaster and York respectively, emphasising the union of the rival houses. The *Matthew* figurehead is an amalgam of the various heraldic symbols – the white greyhound carries a green and white shield displaying the crown and the Tudor rose.

THE SHIP'S BELL

The association of a bell and a ship goes back centuries and the bell played a key role in the day-to-day life on board.

Clocks did not successfully go to sea until the mid-18th century and the passage and regulation of time at sea was based on the local noon, ie, that point during the day when the sun is at its zenith. From this event, the passage of time was measured in 30 or 60 minute periods using a sand glass – a giant egg timer! At the end of each 30 minutes, the sand glass would be inverted to measure the following 30 minutes – and so on.

Using the *Matthew* with her crew of 18 plus the skipper as an example, it was customary to divide the crew into 3 groups with up to 5 or 6 hands per team – each team is called a "watch" and they would spend a 4 hour period "on watch" (steering, lookout, sail trimming). Each 30 minutes of the watch, the bell would be rung: one bell at the end of the first 30 minutes, two bells at the end of 1 hour and so on up to a maximum of 8 bells at the end of the 4th hour. It was not just a case of ringing the bell – there was a sort of code. For instance, at 4 bells, the hand would sound two doubles: two rings, space, two rings. For 7 bells, it would be three doubles and a single. This code ensured that there was no confusion between the watch bells and perhaps other requirements to ring the bell.

At the sounding of the 8 bells, the watch on deck would be relieved by the next watch and so on during the 24 hour day. So each hand would have 4 hour on watch followed by 8 hours sleeping and eating. The pattern of the bell ringing would restart at the beginning of each 4 hour period, ie, the maximum number of bells is 8 (4 doubles). The practice of using a bell continued right up to the 20th century, despite the introduction of clocks during the 18th century. Even at anchor, when a reduced watch of 3 or 4 hands would form an "anchor watch", the practice of announcing each 30 minute period would continue.

Collisions at sea or at a mooring were always a hazard especially in poor visibility and thus the bell could act as a warning to other ships in the immediate vicinity.

FOOD AND WATER

The *Matthew* of today has a fully equipped galley down below. In the 15th century, the luxuries of a gas cooker, refrigeration, canned and freeze-dried food products, were not available and thus the variety of food was limited and in a ship the size of the *Matthew*, all cooking had to be carried out on the main deck because of the potential fire hazard between decks.

Cabot provisioned the ship for a six month passage. A seaman's typical daily diet consisted of 1lb of ship's biscuit, 2lb of salt beef and eight pints of beer, with dried fish and heavily salted butter sometimes taking place of the beef. Water was also carried, with that taken from Bristol's springs on Jacob's Wells Road being renowned for its purity right up to Nelson's time. When the water casks ran low, they were topped up with rain water.

After the first week of any sea voyage, the only fresh food came from any animals carried on board such as goats and chickens to provide milk, eggs or meat, or from fish caught at sea. On Cabot's 1497 voyage this included the codfish the sailors caught on the rich fisheries that lay off the coast of Newfoundland.

Scurvy had not really been encountered because the lengths of the coastal passages were relatively small when compared with the longer voyages of the 16th century and later. Apples, plums and pears, whilst part of the initial provisions, are perishable.

In addition to cooking cauldrons, smaller higher quality pots were also necessary along with cooking dishes made out of redware, stoneware, pottery, iron, and bronze. Other tools, such as cooking knives and a bronze mortar were also necessary. Most of the food was likely boiled and food preparation may have included toasting, grilling or frying.

Knives, forks and spoons with which we are familiar today were not readily available. They ate with their fingers, using their knives to cut and spear their food. Plates and drinking vessels were made of wood (they were unbreakable) and in some cases if a shipwright was amongst the crew, they would carve their own.

CLASSIFICATION

According to National Historic Ships UK, the *Matthew* should be regarded as an 'operational hypothesis'. This is because the ship was the subject of considered research from limited information to determine its form and characteristics as closely as possible to the medieval *Matthew*, but was adapted to meet challenging operational demands - ie extended sea voyages requiring modern navigational equipment, engines and other present day features.

Writing in 2012, Martyn Heighton who was head of Historic Ships UK at the time said, "A good example of an operational hypothesis is *Matthew*, designed by Colin Mudie, in which he called on records which were able to indicate capacity with accuracy (50 tuns), crew numbers (which suggested the kind of rig employed), and the known characteristics of vessels of this period from documentation and contemporary models. All these sources helped Colin Mudie to define the vessel's design."

An 'operational hypothesis' is a bit of a mouthful, but the *Matthew* is definitely an operational sailing ship. Although she's neither a 'replica' nor a 'reconstruction', The Matthew of Bristol Trust is happy to call her a 'faithful representation' of the medieval *Matthew* sailed by Cabot.

OWNERS

2012 to present – The Matthew of Bristol Trust – Owned by the Trust, managed by Matthew (Ventures) Limited and operated by Wakeham Marine Ltd
2006 to 2012 – SS Great Britain Trust – Owned by Trust, managed and operated under licence by Ship Shape and Bristol Fashion Ltd
2002 to 2006 – SS Great Britain Trust – Owned, managed and operated by the Trust
1996 to 2002 – John Cabot's Matthew Trust – Owned, managed and operated by the Trust
1990 to 1996 – Bristol Cabot 500 Celebrations (1997) Ltd

SKIPPERS

2013 to present – Rick Wakeham
2006 to 2012 – Rob Salvidge
2000 to 2005 – Nigel Ottley
1998 to 1999 – Mark Chislett (Shore Captain)
1995 to 1998 – David Alan-Williams

THE MATTHEW IN NUMBERS

SHIP TYPE:
CARAVEL

CREW (INCLUDING SKIPPER):
19

MASTS:
3 (PLUS BOWSPRIT)

LENGTH (INCLUDING CASTLE):
22.25M (73 FEET)

LENGTH (HULL):
19.48M (63 FEET 11 INCHES)

LENGTH (WATERLINE):
18.75M (61 FEET 6 INCHES)

BEAM (HULL):
5.99M (19 FEET 8 INCHES)

BEAM (OVERALL):
6.25M (20 FEET 6 INCHES)

DRAFT:
2.13M (7 FEET)

AIR DRAFT (WITHOUT TOPMAST):
18.59M (61 FEET)

AIR DRAFT (INCLUDING TOPMAST):
21.64M (71 FEET)

DISPLACEMENT LOADED (AND UNLOADED):
77.5 TONS (85 TONS)

SAIL AREA:
219.25 M^2 (2360 FEET^2)

REGISTERED TONNAGE:
58.38 TONS

CRUISING SPEED (POWER):
6 KNOTS (FLAT WATER)

CRUISING SPEED (SAIL):
4 KNOTS

BALLAST (ORIGINALLY STORED THROUGH THE BILGE):
28 TONS

KEEL WEIGHT:
1.5 TONS

TIMBER TYPES & STATS:

KEEL & KEELSON:	OPEPE (AFRICAN HARDWOOD)
FRAMES AND FUTTOCKS:	ENGLISH OAK
UNDERWATER PLANKING:	LARCH
TOPSIDE PLANKING:	DOUGLAS FIR
DECK PLANKING:	DOUGLAS FIR
COVERING BOARDS:	IROKO
BEAMS:	OPEPE

MAIN MAST: DOUGLAS FIR
20.12M (66 FEET)

2.5 TONS AND 75 FEET (UNCUT) WHEN ARRIVED IN BRISTOL. A GIFT FROM THE DUKE OF EDINBURGH FROM THE BALMORAL ESTATE

26 OAK TREES
USED IN BUILDING THE MATTHEW

ACROSS 30 SHIP PARTS
MORE THAN 60M^3
(1800 CUBIC FEET) OF CUTTING WAS CARRIED OUT BY THE SHIPWRIGHTS AT A COST OF
AROUND £40,000

PLANKING TOOK:
3200 NAILS

Tributes and Acknowledgements

What is fascinating from leafing through archive collections, scanning media coverage and talking to individuals is just how many people have a deep affection for the *Matthew* and have played some part in her story. She has been and continues to be a large part of so many people's lives and their pasts. With the passage of time, sadly, many are no longer with us.

Martyn Heighton, who came up with the idea to build the ship when he was Director of Arts at Bristol City Council in the late 1980s, passed away in November 2016. Shortly before he died he shared his memories and commented on the early chapters where his help was very much appreciated. When he left Bristol in 1997 he took up the post of Chief Executive of the Mary Rose Trust and for 12 years was also a Trustee of the *SS Great Britain*. When he died he was Director of National Historic Ships UK and was regarded as the mainstay of the maritime heritage community in the country.

St John Hartnell, who died in 2005, was the key driving force behind The Matthew Project in the 1990s. Without his passion and determination as Chairman, the *Matthew* might never have been built. He put in place the organisation to deliver the project and was able to persuade Michael Slade and Helical Bar plc to underwrite the costs. Without Michael Slade's involvement and vision the project might also have foundered.

Mike Blackwell, who project managed the construction, has also passed away. He was regarded with much affection by the shipwrights who built the *Matthew* - Warwick Moreton, Brian Cumby, Tim Miles, Mark Rolt, Steve Blake, Neil Blake, Denis Williams, Peter Williams, Robert Williams, Douglas Doule, Andy King, Alan Wood, and John Douglas – some of whom are also no longer with us.

The 300-plus members of the former Matthew Society should also be acknowledged for their enthusiasm and support. Its founder Steve Isaacs and secretary Jean Fletcher, were tenacious advocates for the ship and the contribution and passion of other early members and volunteers like Arnold Pick, Mike Lear, Ron Hodges, John Hoskins and Brenda Horwood should also be mentioned.

Unfortunately there's not space to list all the people who have played a part in the *Matthew* story however, it is fitting to pay tribute to today's custodians – The Matthew of Bristol Trust, Wakeham Marine Limited and the skipper and the volunteers who continue to care for the ship and maintain her as an operational visitor attraction.

Special thanks to Bristol Archives for providing access to the vast array of *Matthew* material held at B Bond Warehouse in collection RefNo 44086.

In no particular order, grateful thanks also go to the following who have helped enormously with information, stories, anecdotes, images and in many cases as sounding boards during the development and production of this book:

Royston Griffey, Rick Wakeham, Helen Wakeham, Charlotte Rooney, Rowen Mackenzie, Dovile Arlauskaite, Hazel Hatton, Nick Barnfield, Shawn Spencer-Smith, Dr Evan Jones, Rodney North, Mary North, Chris LeGrow, Mark Chislett, Paul Venton, John Wilson, Colin Coombs, Nicholas King, Roger Gough, Ann May, Joe Burt, Graham Tratt, Matt Coles, Malcolm Boyns, Julian Warren, David Emeney, Hannah Cunnliffe and Victoria Wallworth at National Historic Ships UK, the Maritime Museum, Rotterdam, David Alan-Williams, Laurel Alan-Williams, and David Redfern.

Picture Credits

Front Cover – Nick Barnfield
Endpapers – Colin Coombs
Back Cover – Matthew of Bristol Trust
p9 – Shawn Spencer-Smith
p10 – Bristol Museum and Art Gallery
p12 – top – Painting by Thomson. From J.A. Cochrane, The Story of Newfoundland. (Montreal: Ginn and Co., 1938) 29.
p12 – bottom – Kids Britannica. The Granger Collection, New York
p13 – left – Bristol Archives RefNo 43207/11/29
p13 – right – Clive Burlton
p14 – left – Colin Coombs
p14 – right – Clive Burlton
p15 – left – Bristol Archives RefNo 19818/1
p16 – Guy Harris/National Historic Ships UK
p18 – Clive Burlton
p19 – Mike Blackwell RefNo 44086
p20 – Sandra Voogt/Maritime Museum Rotterdam
p21 – The Mary Rose Museum
p22 – sketch from the 1483 book *Die Reise ins Heilige Land*, by Bernahard von Breydenbach
p23 – left – Colin Mudie research papers showing the stern of a caravel and the triangular lateen-sail. From a German woodcut, 1486.
P23 – right – Sketch from Libre de cosolat tractat dels fets maritims, Barcelona 1502
p24 – the *Nuremberg Chronicle*, written by Hartmann Schedel with woodcut illustrations by Michael Wolgemut, 1493
p25 – from Colin Mudie's plans of the *Matthew*

p26 to p33 - Mike Blackwell RefNo 44086
p34 – Jean Fletcher RefNo 44086
p35 – Terry Nash RefNo 44086
p36 to p38 – Mike Blackwell RefNo 44086
p39 – Clive Burlton
p40 – Mike Blackwell RefNo 44086
p41 – Jean Fletcher RefNo 44086
p42 & p43 – David Redfern RefNo 44086
p44 – map drawn by Joe Burt
p45 – top – Mike Blackwell RefNo 44086
p45 – bottom – Jean Fletcher RefNo 44086
p46 – left - Matthew of Bristol Trust
p46 – right – Terry Nash RefNo 44086
p47 – Jean Fletcher RefNo 44086
p48 – Chris LeGrow
p49 – David Redfern RefNo 44086
p50 – David Redfern RefNo 44086
p51 – Chris LeGrow
p52 – Jean Fletcher RefNo 44086
p53 – left – David Redfern RefNo 44086
p53 – right – Jean Fletcher RefNo 44086
p54 – top – Jean Fletcher RefNo 44086
p54 – bottom – Mark Chislett
p55 – Mark Chislett
p56 – Chris LeGrow
p57 – Chris LeGrow
p58 – map drawn by Joe Burt
p59 – Mark Chislett
p61 – Chris LeGrow
p62 – David Redfern RefNo 44086
p63 – Chris LeGrow
p65 – Chris LeGrow
p66 – Chris LeGrow
p67 – Chris LeGrow
p68 – Chris LeGrow
p69 – Chris LeGrow
p71 – Chris LeGrow
p72 - Chris LeGrow

p73 - Chris LeGrow
p75 – David Redfern RefNo 44086
p76 – David Redfern RefNo 44086
p78 – Chris LeGrow
p79 – David Redfern RefNo 44086
p80 – map drawn by Joe Burt
p81 – David Redfern RefNo 44086
p82 – David Redfern RefNo 44086
p83 – David Redfern RefNo 44086
p84 – David Redfern RefNo 44086
p85 – David Redfern RefNo 44086
p86 – David Redfern RefNo 44086
p87 – David Redfern RefNo 44086
p88 – Rodney & Mary North
p89 – David Redfern RefNo 44086
p90 – Mark Chislett
p91 – David Redfern RefNo 44086
p92 – Mark Chislett
P93 – Mark Chislett
p94 – Mark Chislett
p95 – Mark Chislett
p97 – top left – Shawn Spencer-Smith
p97 – top right – Mark Chislett
p97 – lower – Mark Chislett
p98 – Nick Barnfield
p99 – Shawn Spencer-Smith
p100 – Lenny George
p101 – top – Shawn Spencer-Smith
p101 – bottom – Joe Burt
p102 – Colin Coombs
p103 – Shawn Spencer-Smith
p104 - Olivier Burnside
p105 – Shawn Spencer-Smith
p106 – Shawn Spencer-Smith
p107 – top left - Ian Skriczka
p107 – top right - Colin Coombs
p107 – bottom right - Colin Coombs

115

Interested in Volunteering?

Visitors to the *Matthew* are greeted and guided around the ship by volunteers from RSVP West - a region of the Retired and Senior Volunteer Programme that is part of the national volunteering charity, Volunteering Matters. RSVP West first started to provide support when the *Matthew* was under construction at Redcliffe Wharf where enthusiastic volunteers helped to staff the Visitor Information Centre during the mid-1990s.

Today, volunteers help to maintain the ship and crew her on daily and evening excursions and on longer sailings. The guide crew comprises around 30 men and women, and are organised across a six-days-a-week watch rota to help visitors enjoy and appreciate the unique qualities of the ship.

Volunteers who become members of the crew are literally taught the ropes and are given other specialist instruction, including first aid, fire drill and how to cope with emergencies such as somebody falling overboard – thankfully that hasn't happened yet!

Volunteers commit themselves to at least one half-day a week, morning or afternoon, and a key skill is enjoying talking to people.

More volunteers are always needed. As older members retire or leave, new ones are regularly needed to help keep the ship's busy schedule fully staffed. It's not necessary for new volunteers to know the intricacies of sailing ships as training will be given.

Interested in volunteering? In the first instance contact the Office and Marketing team by telephone, **0117 927 6868**, or email **info@matthew.co.uk**.

Visitor Information

The *Matthew*'s sailing season is between early March and late November. During this time visitors are offered free tours on board as well as pre-booked trips around the harbour and beyond.

PUBLIC TRIPS

Harbour Cruise – 1 hour
Soak up the atmosphere of Bristol's historic Floating Harbour during this one hour trip.

Captain Barnacle's Pirate Panto – 1 hour
A perfect trip for both children and their parents. Join legendary Captain Barnacle the Bristol pirate for a rip-roaring trip aboard the *Matthew*.

Cream Tea Cruise – 1.5 hours
Experience the city from the water and indulge in a traditional cream tea and a hot drink.

Fish and Chips Trip – 2 hours
Enjoy a traditional meal of fish and chips during this leisurely afternoon or evening cruise around the harbour.

Sea Shanty Fish and Chips Trip – 2 hours
Like the fish and chips trips above, but better! Enjoy a meal while listening to a live musical accompaniment from one of the *Matthew*'s resident sea shanty bands.

Avon Gorge Trip – 3-4 hours
Experience the fantastic views of the Avon Gorge passing beneath the Clifton Suspension Bridge and down the River Avon to Pill and back.

Private Hire
The *Matthew* offers a unique venue for a variety of occasions - regularly hosting private charters including wedding receptions, birthday parties, work parties, reunions, and corporate events.

HOW TO FIND THE MATTHEW

The ship is moored alongside the M Shed museum:
Prince's Wharf
Wapping Road
Bristol
BS1 4RN

On Foot: The *Matthew* is a 5 to 10-minute walk from the city centre or a 20-minute walk from Temple Meads train station.
Public transport: Any bus with a City Centre drop off. Visit the Travelwest website for bus routes.
Ferry: Ferries are available from Temple Meads, Hotwells, and the Centre to Prince Street Bridge.
Car: Two miles from the M32. The Grove, Wapping Wharf, and *SS Great Britain* car parks are located nearby.

OPENING HOURS

10am to 4pm Tuesdays to Sundays. If making a special visit, please call to check that the ship is not on a trip.
Visit the website or get in touch for more information, prices, and to book tickets online:

www.matthew.co.uk
info@matthew.co.uk
Telephone: **0117 927 6868**

Connect with the *Matthew* on social media – images and comments are welcome.
Facebook: **@TheMatthewBristol**
Twitter: **@TheMatthewShip**
Instagram: **@matthew1497**

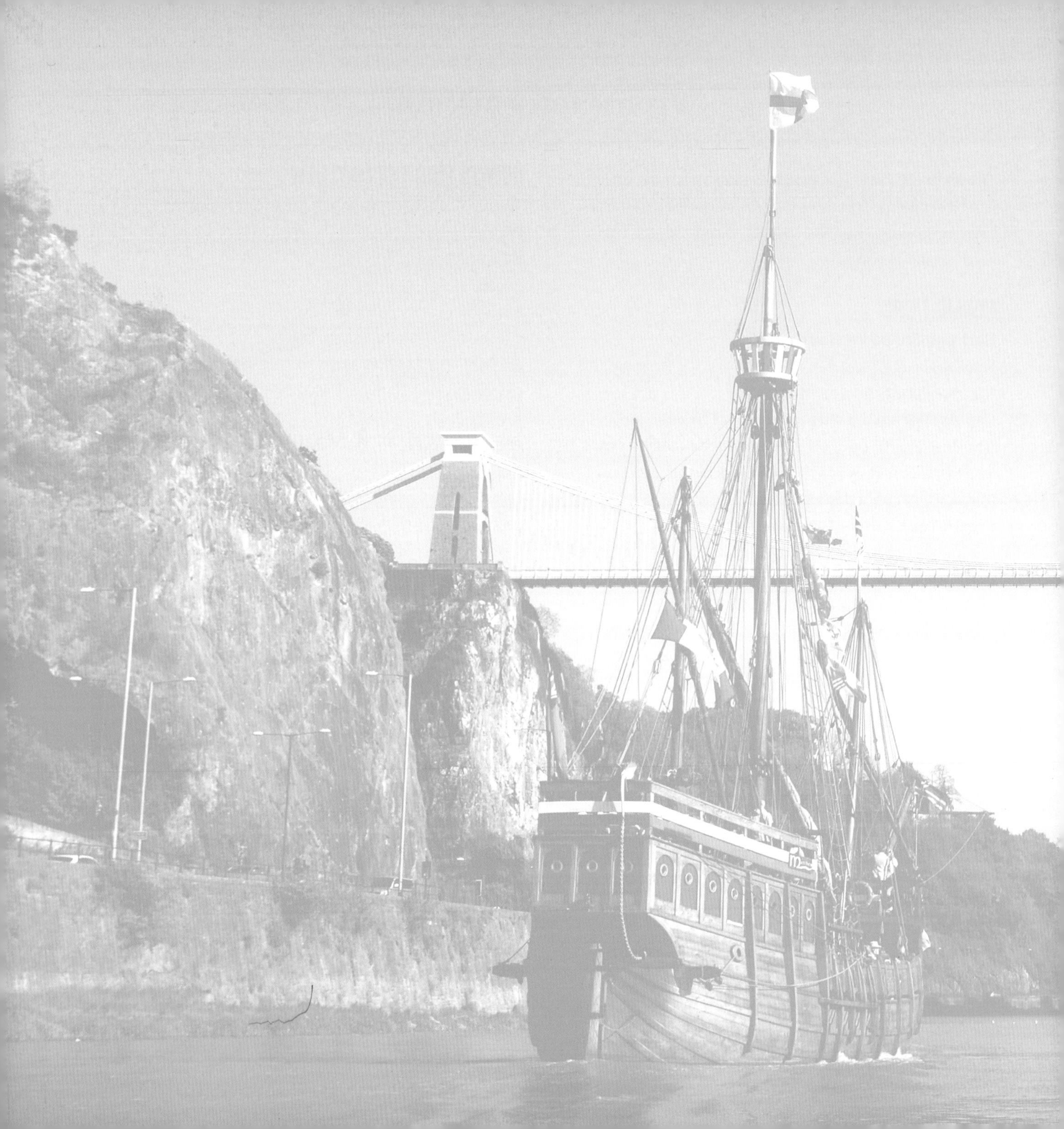